Word 2016 Level 2
Student Edition

30 Bird Media
510 Clinton Square
Rochester NY 14604
www.30Bird.com

Word 2016 Level 2

Student Edition

CEO, 30 Bird Media: Adam A. Wilcox

Series designed by: Clifford J. Coryea, Donald P. Tremblay, and Adam A Wilcox

Managing Editor: Donald P. Tremblay

Instructional Design Lead: Clifford J. Coryea

Copyeditor: Robert S. Kulik

Keytester: Kurt J. Specht

COPYRIGHT © 2016 30 Bird Media LLC. All rights reserved

No part of this work may be reproduced or used in any other form without the prior written consent of the publisher.

Visit www.30bird.com for more information.

Trademarks

Some of the product names and company names used in this book have been used for identification purposes only and may be trademarks or registered trademarks of their respective manufacturers and sellers.

Disclaimer

We reserve the right to revise this publication without notice.

WORD2016-L2-R20-SCB

Table of Contents

Introduction 1
    Course setup 2

Chapter 1: Shapes, WordArt, and SmartArt 3
    Module A: Shapes and text 4
    Module B: SmartArt 14

Chapter 2: Managing documents 21
    Module A: Custom themes 22
    Module B: Building blocks 30
    Module C: Section breaks 35
    Module D: Page backgrounds 43

Chapter 3: Styles 53
    Module A: Character styles 54
    Module B: Paragraph styles 70

Chapter 4: References and hyperlinks 77
    Module A: Reference notes 78
    Module B: Table of contents 83
    Module C: Hyperlinks 101

Chapter 5: Navigation and organization 107
    Module A: Navigating documents 108
    Module B: Master documents 115

Chapter 6: Saving and sharing documents 121
    Module A: Saving and sending 122
    Module B: Comments 140
    Module C: Protecting documents 146

Alphabetical Index 155

Introduction

Welcome to *Word 2016 Level 2*. This course provides the concepts and skills to use some more advanced features of Microsoft Word 2016, including enhanced formatting, references, editing, and sharing, and saving to various formats. This course, and the two others in this series, map to the objectives of the Microsoft Office Specialist and Expert exams for Word 2016. Objective coverage is marked throughout the course, and you can download an objectives map for the series from http://www.30bird.com.

You will benefit most from this course if you want to accomplish advanced workplace tasks in Word 2016, or if you want to have a solid foundation for continuing on to become a Word Expert. If you intend to take a Microsoft Office Core or Expert exam for Word, this course is a good place to start your preparation, but you will need to continue on to the last course in the series to be fully prepared for either exam.

The course assumes you know how to use a computer, and that you're familiar with Microsoft Windows and the basics of Microsoft Word.

After you complete this course, you will know how to:

- Insert and format shapes and text boxes, and insert and format SmartArt diagrams
- Create custom themes, use building blocks and section breaks, and apply page backgrounds
- Insert footnotes and endnotes, insert a table of contents, and apply hyperlinks
- Edit a document for spelling and grammar, navigate a large document, and use master documents and subdocuments
- Save documents in various sharable formats, add and manage comments, and protect a document from unwanted changes

This is the second course in this series. After you complete it, consider going on to the last:

- *Word 2016: Level 3*

Course setup

To complete this course, each student and instructor will need to have a computer running Word 2016. Setup instructions and activities are written assuming Windows 10; however, with slight modification the course will work using Windows XP Service Pack 3, Windows Vista Service Pack 1, Windows 7, or Windows 8.x.

Hardware requirements for Windows 10 course setup include:

- 1 GHz or faster processor
- 2 GB RAM
- 25 GB total hard drive space (50 GB or more recommended)
- DirectX 10 (or later) video card or integrated graphics, with a minimum of 128 MB of graphics memory
- Monitor with 1280x800 or higher resolution
- Wi-Fi or Ethernet adapter

Software requirements include:

- Windows 10 (or alternative, as above)
- Microsoft Word 2016 or any Microsoft Office 2016 edition
- The Word 2016 Level 2 data files and PowerPoint slides, available at http://www.30bird.com
- An email application and a working email account for a single exercise in one chapter on attaching a workbook to an email (which can instead be skipped or demonstrated by the instructor)

Network requirements include:

- An Internet connection to use online templates and images (which can instead be skipped or demonstrated by the instructor)

Because the exercises in this course include viewing and changing some Word defaults, it's recommended to begin with a fresh installation of the software. But this is certainly not necessary. Just be aware that if you are not using a fresh installation, some exercises might work slightly differently, and some screens might look slightly different.

 Note: Opening downloaded files in Office applications can result in the document being displayed in Protected view. This can be overridden by clicking **Enable Editing** at the top of the document window.

1. Install Windows 10, including all recommended updates and service packs. Use a different computer and user name for each student.
2. Install Microsoft Word 2016 or Office 2016, using all defaults during installation.
3. Update Word or Office using Windows Update.
4. Copy the Word 2016 Level 2 data files to the Documents folder.

Chapter 1: Shapes, WordArt, and SmartArt

You will learn how to:

- Insert shapes and use WordArt
- Insert and format SmartArt

Module A: Shapes and text

You can add different shapes to your Word document, combine several shapes to make more complex shapes, and edit and format shapes after they are inserted.

You will learn how to:

- Insert a shape
- Modify shape borders
- Apply shape styles
- Add text to shapes and apply WordArt

Inserting shapes

Unlike a picture or clip art, a shape does not go in as a character. By default, it's drawn on top of any exiting text.

 Exam Objective: MOS Word Core 5.1.1

1. On the Insert tab, click **Shapes**.
   To open the shapes gallery.

2. Select the shape you want to create.
   The gallery closes, and the pointer resembles a large plus sign.

3. Drag on the document where you want the shape to be.
   To keep the original aspect ratio, hold **Shift** while you drag.
   The shape is drawn on the document.

4. To move the shape, point to an edge, but *not* on a handle, and drag it where you want.

Once the shape is in place, you can edit its size, shape, and location in many ways. Use the **Position** and **Wrap Text** commands to change the way the shape interacts with surrounding text.

Modifying shape borders

There are a number of ways to modify the path of a shape's border after you've inserted it. First, select the shape, if necessary, by clicking it. Then, click the **Drawing Tools Format** tab.

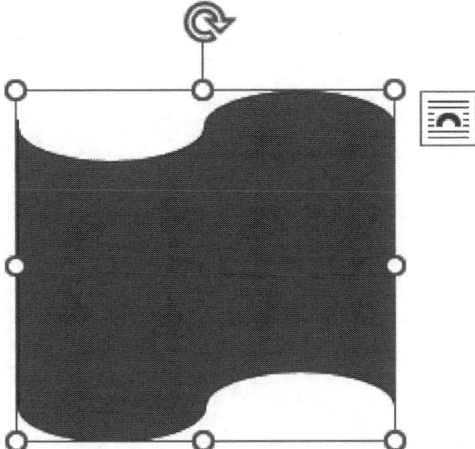

- To resize the shape, drag the corner or edge handles. To preserve the aspect ratio, hold down **Shift** while dragging a corner handle.
- To rotate the shape, drag the rotation handle around. It's the circular arrow.
- Some shapes also have yellow handles to resize certain parts of the shape.
- On the Drawing Tools Format tab, in the Insert Shapes group, click **Edit Shape > Change Shape** to select a different shape from the gallery.
    The new shape will replace the old in the same bounding box; that is, at the same location, size, and rotation.
- In the Insert Shapes group, click **Edit Shape > End Points**.
    Black square handles appear along the path of the border. The more complicated the path, the more handles there are.

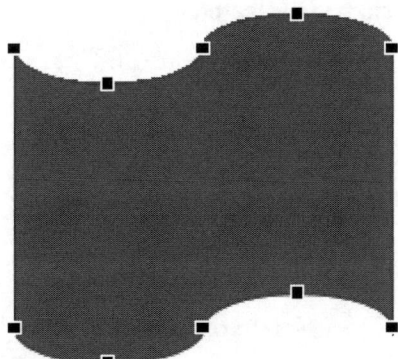

- Drag the endpoint handles to change the shape.
- Drag any point on the border to create a new point and change the shape.
- When you click (or drag) a point, two lines with white handles appear on either side. Drag these to control the shape of the curve on that side of the point.

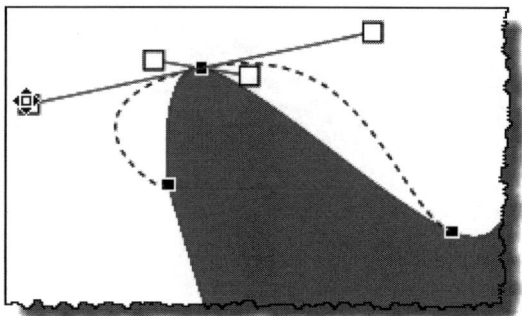

- Right-click a point to see a menu of other options for adding, removing, and changing points, as well as the micro formatting toolbar.

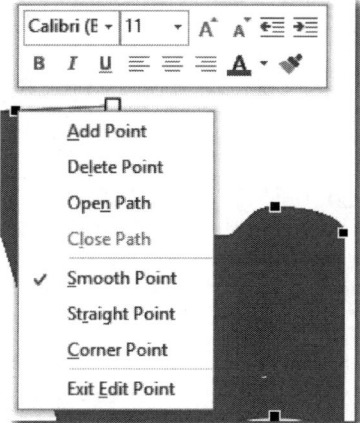

The best way to learn about adjusting points and curves is to experiment.

Shape styles

After you insert a shape, you can apply various styles to it by using the options in the Shape Styles group on the Drawing Tools Format tab. This tab becomes available when a shape is selected.

A shape's style is the combination of three general attributes:

- *Shape Fill* is the color and gradient of the fill. You can also use a picture or texture image as fill.
- *Shape Outline* is the color, thickness, and dash pattern of the border.
- *Shape Effects* are special effects like shadow, bevel, and 3-D rotation.

You can choose from the shape styles gallery to apply several of these attributes at once, or you can apply your own combination. The figure shows the same shape, a rounded rectangle, with the default formatting (left) and with a different color and effects applied: reflection, bevel, shadow, and 3-D rotation. You can also use the format painter to copy a shape's style and apply it to another shape.

The menu commands will suffice for much of what you want to do, but if you need more precise control over shape effects, right-click a shape and click **Format Shape**. You can also use the dialog box launcher in the Shape Styles group. This opens the Format Shape pane, in which you can, for example, expand the Fill and/or Line options to set angles of rotation, transparency of reflections, and the details of beveled and reflective shapes. You can leave the Format Shape pane open as you select different shapes.

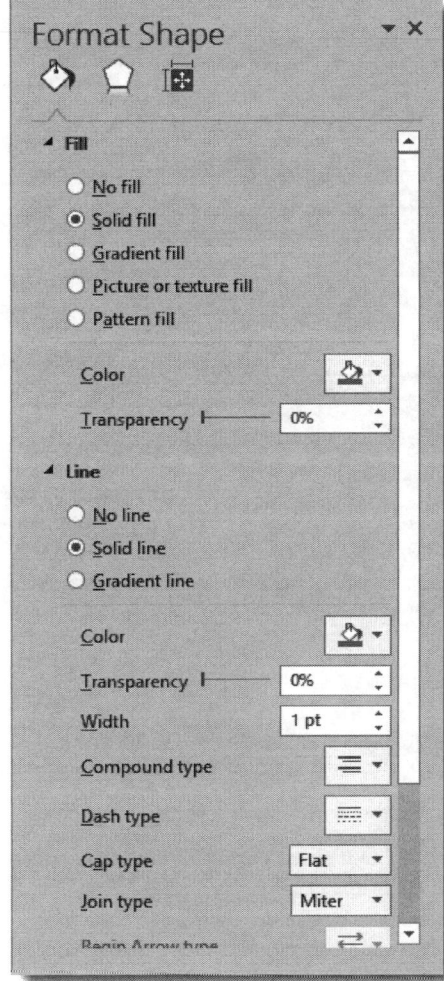

Exercise: Inserting a shape

Do This	How & Why
1. Start a new, blank document, and save it as Shapes.	
2. On the Insert tab, click **Shapes** and select a rectangle shape with rounded or clipped corners.	Pick any rectangle except a simple one. The pointer changes into a large plus sign.
3. Drag a rectangle that's about 2 in x 4 in (5cm x 10 cm).	
4. Experiment with dragging different handles and edges. • Corner handles adjust size while maintaining aspect ratio. • Side handles change size and aspect ratio. • Yellow handles, when present, change characteristics of curves and angles. • The round, white handle freely rotates the shape.	
5. On the Format tab, experiment with various shape effects.	Try changing the shadow, reflection, bevel, and rotation, and whatever else you want.
6. Experiment with other shapes and effects, as time allows.	If time allows. Right-click a shape, and click **Format Shape**. Experiment with the options in this pane.
7. Save and close the document.	

Text on shapes

To place text on a shape, select the shape and start typing.

If at first you don't like the way it looks, don't worry about it; you can adjust it. For one thing, you can select text on a shape and then use font and paragraph options on the Home tab, just as you would with any text.

Also, when text on a shape is selected, the Drawing Tools Format tab appears, which contains the WordArt Styles and Text groups.

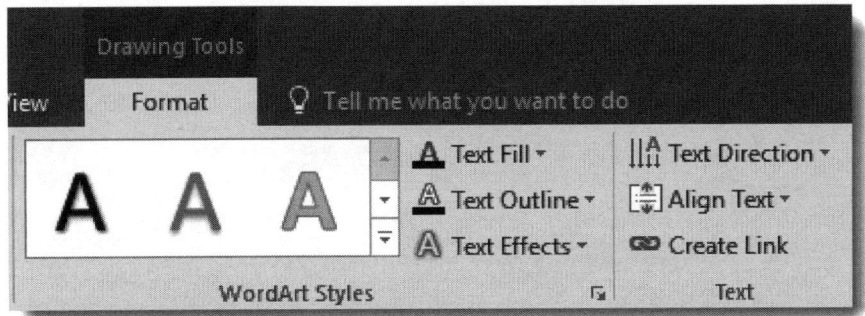

- The **Text Direction** command allows you to make the text run vertically, so that it runs up or down the page. This is useful, for instance, for having a section title along the edge of the page.

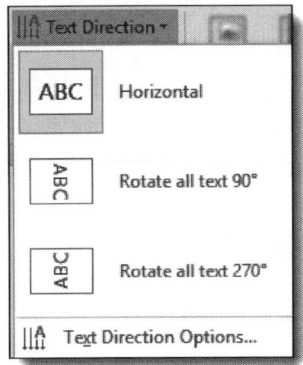

- The **Align Text** command aligns the text within the shape—top, middle, or bottom. For other text alignment options, use the paragraph group on the Home tab.

- The **Create Link** command allows you to link text boxes, so that text can run from one text box to another. This is not to be confused with creating hyperlinks.

Inserting text boxes

It is helpful to remember that there is no difference in Word between a shape and a text box. A text box is a shape with text on it. Some text boxes have the text in a container, but the box is still a shape.

 Exam Objective: MOS Word Core 5.1.4

There are several ways to insert a text box.

- In the Insert tab, click **Shapes**, then click the text box icon in the shapes gallery.
  It's under Basic Shapes.

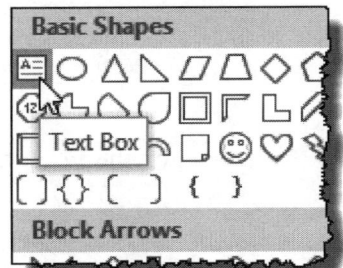

- Select any shape, and enter text.
- On the Insert tab, click **WordArt**, and then select a style.
  This creates a text box with formatted text.

- On the Insert tab, click **Text Box**, and then select a text box from the gallery.
    It contains text boxes that have been formatted and positioned for various purposes.
- On the Drawing Tools Format tab, in the Insert Shapes group, click the down arrow to the right of the shapes gallery, and then select a text-box shape.

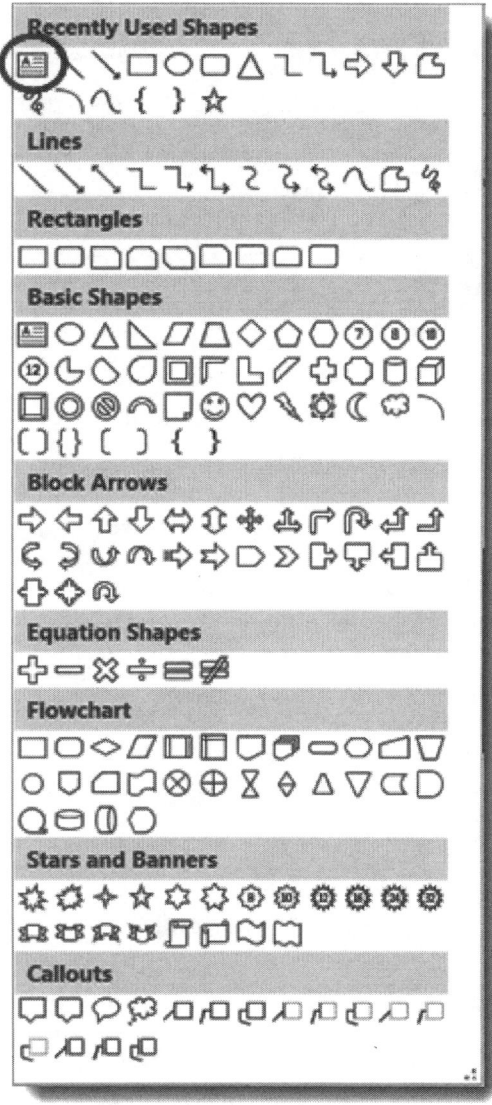

If you want to save the style for a text box that you've created, select the text box, then, on the Insert tab, click **Text Box > Save Selection to Text Box Gallery**.

WordArt

   Exam Objective: MOS Word Core 2.2.10

Text both inside and outside text boxes can be formatted with the font and paragraph options on the Home tab. You can change things like font face, size, color, spacing, and alignment. You can even apply some font effects such as glow and reflection to either text type.

But only text in a text box can receive the full WordArt treatment, which includes 3-D rotation, following a path, and warping. In fact, to change text to WordArt, just apply a WordArt style to text in the document body; the text is then pulled out and put in a text box.

WordArt essentially treats text characters like a set of shapes, and WordArt styles are much like shape styles, with many of the same options. The WordArt group is on the Drawing Tools Format tab, which appears when a shape or text box is selected.

- *Text Fill* is the color and gradient of the text. The gradient is applied across all the text in the box, not each letter.
- *Text Outline* is the color, weight, and dash pattern of the character outlines.
- *Text Effects* include many of the options available for shapes, such as shadow, reflection, glow, bevel, and 3-D rotation. In addition, WordArt has options to transform the text to follow a path or to be warped, as in the figure below.

If you are going to apply both WordArt styles to the text and shape styles to the text box, you'll need to experiment with how the effects work together. For instance, if you reflect the text box, you won't need to reflect the text, because it will already be reflected. Some combinations of text box and text formatting will give you unpleasant results.

Note that you can't use a 3-D rotation for the text that is different than that of the text box. Whichever option you set last applies to both.

Exercise: Using WordArt

Do This	How & Why
1. Start a new, blank document, and save it as `Textbox`.	
2. On the Insert tab, click **Text Box > Draw Text Box**.	
3. Drag a rectangle on the document.	A simple rectangle is drawn with a cursor in it.
4. Type your full name.	Or anything else you want.
5. Increase the font size: a) Select all of the text, or select the shape by clicking its border. b) On the Home tab, change the font size to `36`. c) Resize the shape to fit the text, if necessary. d) Switch back to the Format tab.	
6. In the WordArt Styles group, experiment with Text Effects.	Experiment especially with Transform effects, which apply only to text. Transformed text also has yellow handles which you use to change the transform effect. Also experiment with gradients, under Text Fill.
7. Experiment with other text boxes, as time allows.	See how the Shapes Styles and WordArt Styles interact.
8. Save and close the document.	

Assessment: Shapes and text

1. A text box is a shape with text on it. True or false?
   - True
   - False

2. How can you access the Drawing Tools Format tab?
   - Select a shape.
   - Right-click a shape, and click Format Shape.
   - Press Ctrl+F.

3. Which two ways can you open the Format Shape pane to have precise control over shape effects?
   - Right-click a shape, and click Format Shape.
   - Click the lower-right corner of the Shape Styles group.
   - Double-click a shape.
   - Right-click a shape, and click More Layout Options.

Module B: SmartArt

SmartArt is a set of professionally designed diagrams made up of shapes and text.

You will learn:

- How to insert and format SmartArt

About SmartArt

 Exam Objective: MOS Word Core 5.3.1, 5.3.2, 5.3.3

You add a SmartArt diagram from the Insert tab. The SmartArt gallery is organized by design and purpose. The shapes in SmartArt can hold text, pictures, or both.

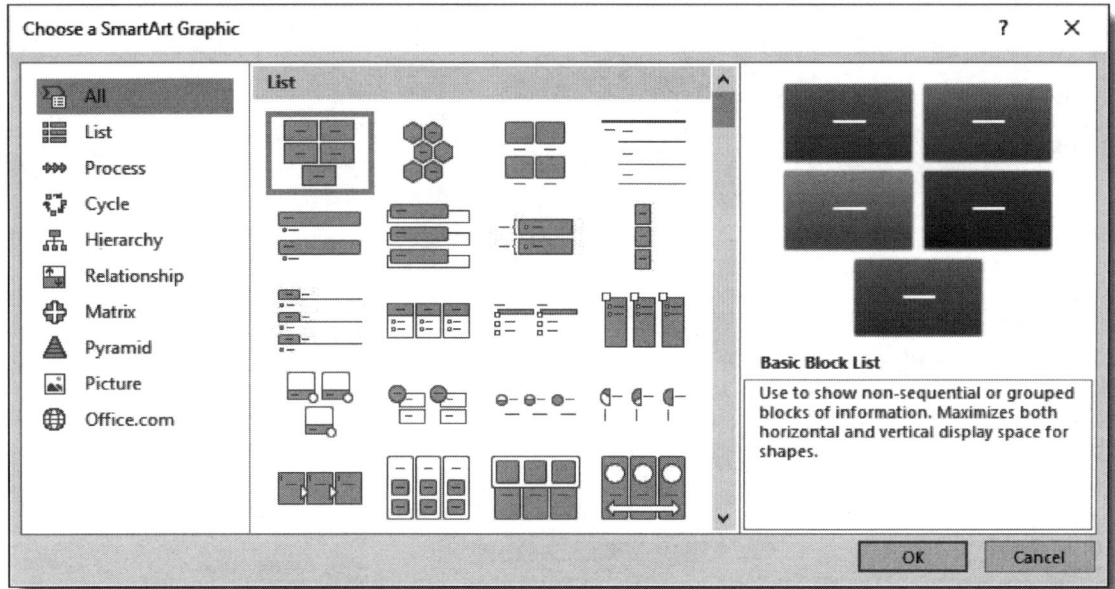

The parts of a SmartArt diagram are inserted into you document in a container that can be moved and resized. When you resize the container, the diagram is resized accordingly.

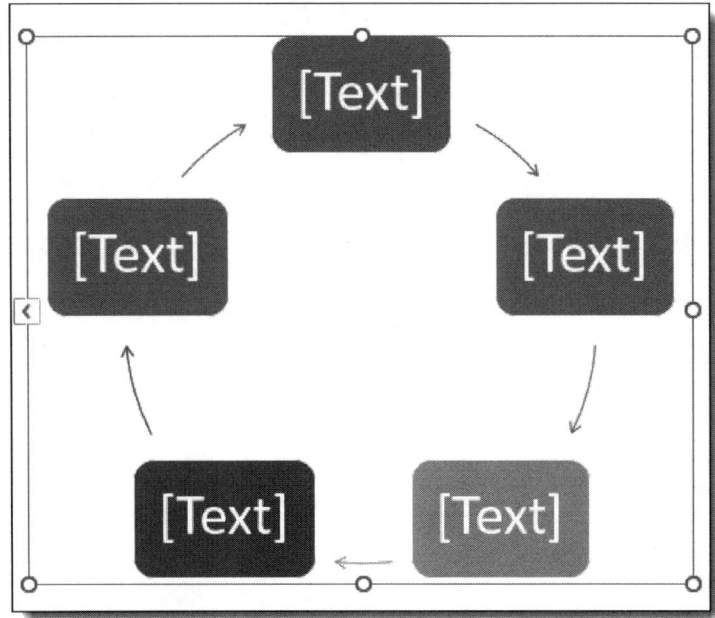

When SmartArt is selected in a document, two related tabs become available: Design and Format. The Design tab has options for the overall layout and color of the diagram. The Format tab has options for shape and WordArt formatting, and is very similar to the Drawing Tools Format tab.

SmartArt formatting

Exam Objective: MOS Word Core 5.3.1, 5.3.2, 5.3.3

You can add text directly to the shapes in a SmartArt diagram, or you can click the expand button on the left edge of the container to open the text pane.

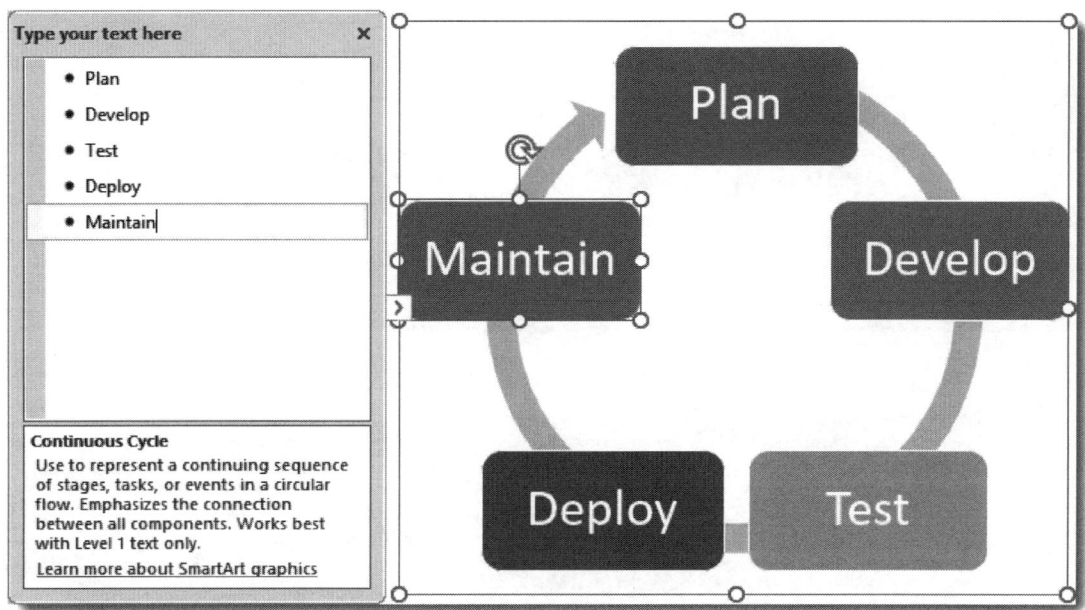

The text pane allows you to indent items, which makes them sub-items of the list item above, and puts them in the same shape.

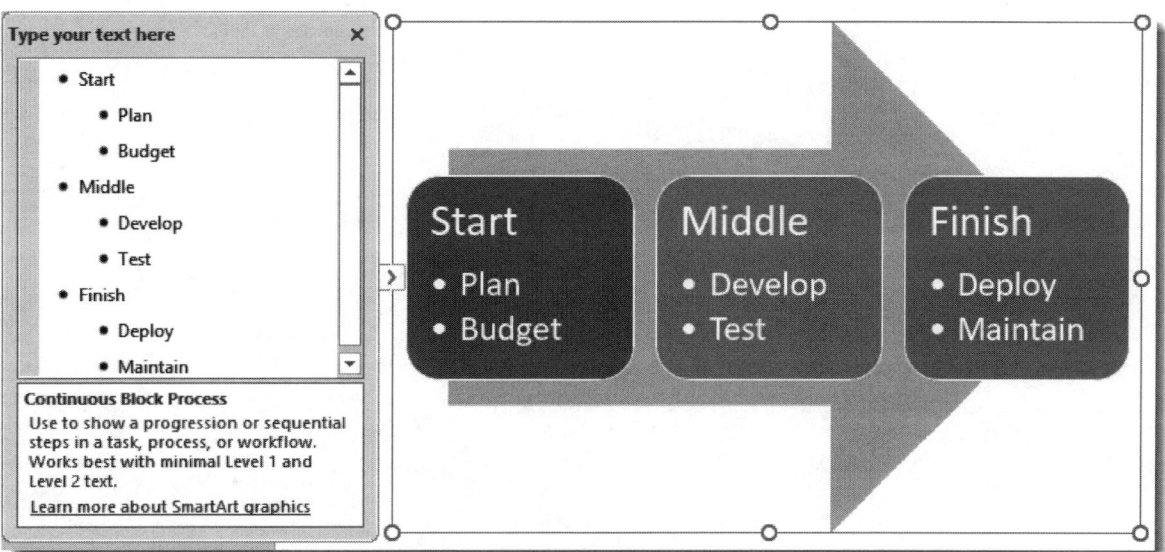

Using the Design tab, you can change the layout and colors of the diagram. The Format tab lets you format the shapes and text using shape styles and WordArt styles. You format shapes in SmartArt just as you would standalone shapes. If you select a single shape in the diagram and then apply shape styles or WordArt styles, the effects are applied only to the selected shape. If you have the whole diagram selected, the shape and WordArt formatting is applied to all parts of the diagram.

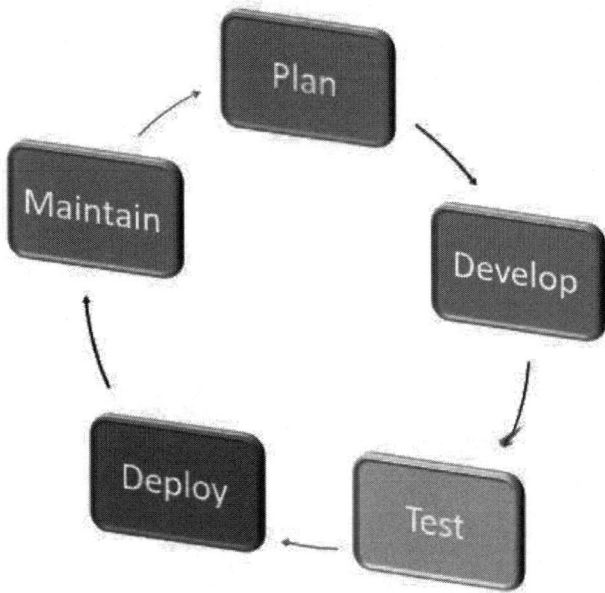

To remove all effects and return to the default formatting, click **Reset Graphic**. This doesn't remove any shapes or text you've added.

Exercise: Inserting SmartArt

Do This	How & Why
1. Start a new blank document, and save it as `SmartArt`.	
2. On the Insert tab, click **SmartArt**.	The Choose a SmartArt Graphic window opens.
3. Look through the graphics for various categories.	
4. In the Cycle category, select **Radial Cycle**, and click **OK**.	The cycle graphic is inserted into a container with the default color.
5. On the SmartArt Design tab, in the Create Graphic group, click **Add Shape**.	To add a circle to the cycle.
6. On the left edge of the graphic container, click the expand button.	

Do This	How & Why
7. Enter the following text in the six bullets: • Development Cycle • Research • Design • Code • Test • Deploy	
8. Close the text entry box.	
9. On the Design tab, click **Change Colors**, and click the first choice under Colorful.	
10. Drag the bottom center of the frame down.	To make the diagram bigger.
11. On the Design tab, in the SmartArt Styles group, select a style of your choosing from the gallery.	You diagram should look something like the figure, depending on which style you chose.
12. Save and close the document.	

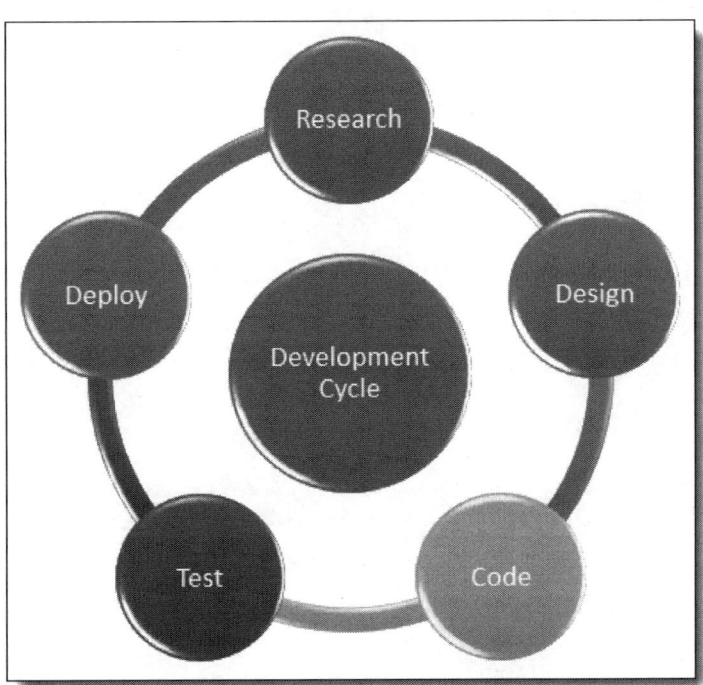

Assessment: SmartArt

1. Clicking Reset Graphic returns a graphic to its original state, immediately after you've inserted it. True or false?

    - True
    - False

2. You can apply different styles to individual shapes in a SmartArt diagram. True or false?

    - True
    - False

Summary: Shapes, WordArt, and SmartArt

You should now know how to:

- Insert shapes, change shape borders and styles, add text to shapes, and apply WordArt
- Insert and format SmartArt

Synthesis: Shapes, WordArt, and SmartArt

1. Start a new, blank document, and save it as `FoodArt`.
2. Insert the SmartArt Bending Picture Caption List.
   It's in the Picture category.

   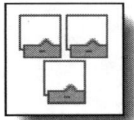

3. Resize the frame, so that there are two shapes over one shape and the graphic is a little larger.
   Drag the bottom down.
4. Add the following text in the text pane:
   - `Specialty Drinks`
   - `Baked Goods`
   - `Sandwiches`
5. Change the color to **Colored Fill - Accent 2**.
   Click **Change Colors**, and click the second orange option.
6. Change the bevel to **Riblet**.
   Use Shape Effects on the Format tab. Ensure that the frame is selected but not any individual shapes.
7. Add a picture to the first shape:
   a) Click the image icon in the center of the first shape.
   b) Click **Browse**.
   c) Select the picture file `Drinks`.
   d) Click **Insert**.
8. Add the pictures `Baked` and `Sandwich` to the other two shapes.
9. De-select the SmartArt frame.
   Your graphic should look something like the figure on the next page.
10. Save and close the file.

Chapter 2: Managing documents

You will learn how to:

- Divide a document using sections
- Insert Quick Parts
- Customize document themes
- Format page backgrounds

Module A: Custom themes

Word comes with a variety of themes you can apply to your documents, but if none of them fits your needs, you can customize one and even save it as a new theme of your own.

You will learn how to:

- Set individual theme elements
- Create new theme fonts and colors
- Save or load themes

Theme elements

A theme consists of three elements, as shown in the Document Formatting group on the Design tab.

Exam Objective: MOS Word Core 4.2.3 and Expert 1.3.2

Colors   A theme has twelve colors. Ten are those you see in the Theme Colors section of the color menus throughout Word. These include lighter and darker variants: one *Light Text/Background*, two *Dark Text/Background*, and six *Accents*. The last two are *Hyperlink* and *Followed Hyperlink*.

Fonts   A theme has two fonts: a heading font and a body font. They can be the same or different.

Effects   Theme effects apply only to graphical elements like shapes, charts, and SmartArt graphics. Beyond that, they're visible only if you format those shapes with theme effects. Although effects are less frequently visible than colors and fonts, they still can make a vivid difference in a document's graphics.

Different theme effects applied to the same shape.

By clicking any of the three galleries, you can set that element independently. By default, each gallery contains an entry for each installed theme. For example, you can use the colors of the *Civic* theme, the fonts of *Black Tie*, and the effects of *Slipstream*.

Remember, when you change a theme or its elements, any formatting that uses colors, fonts, or effects that aren't part of the theme remain unchanged.

- Colors change only if they are from the Theme Colors list. Standard Colors and Custom Colors do not change.
- Fonts change only if they are selected from the Theme Fonts list, either by styles or by manual formatting.
- Shape effects are a little less obvious. They mostly apply to shape styles that contain "Effect" in the name, but this isn't universal. For instance, whether a chart style uses theme effects isn't obvious from its name.

Creating theme colors

Exam Objective: MOS Word Expert 4.2.1

If none of the existing themes has the colors you want, you can create a new set in the Create New Theme Colors window.

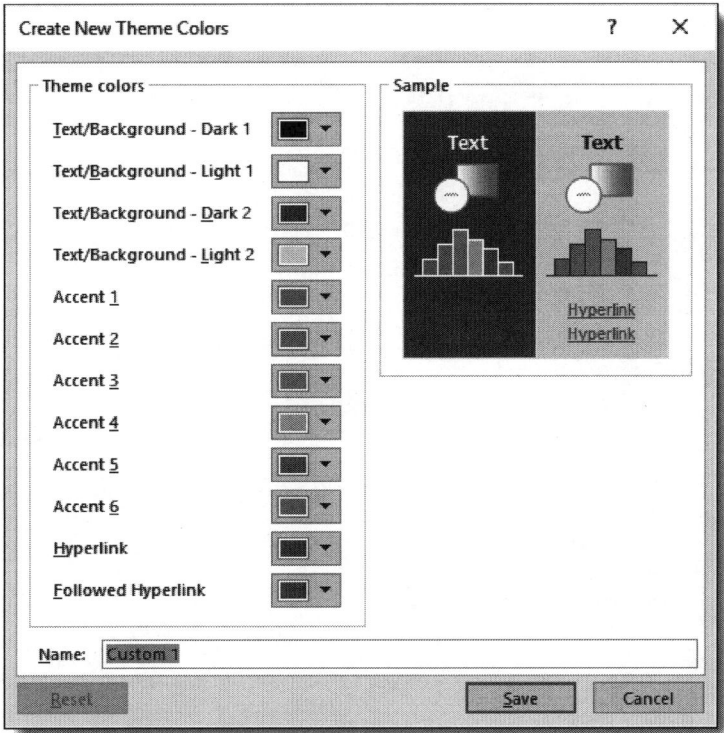

1. Click **Colors > Customize Colors**.
2. Set each theme color.
    If the color you want isn't listed, click **More Colors** to open the Colors window.

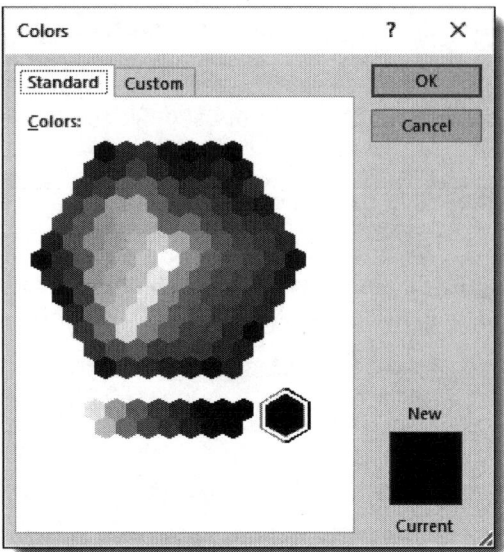

3. Type a name for the new theme color set.
4. Click **Save**.

Creating theme fonts

 Exam Objective: MOS Word Expert 4.2.2

You can choose new theme fonts from the Create New Theme Fonts window.

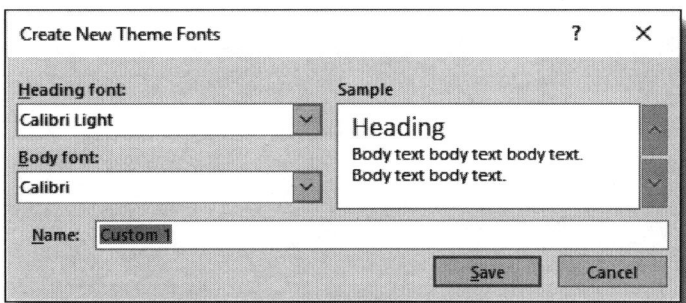

1. Click **Fonts > Customize Fonts**.
   To open the Create New Theme Fonts window.
2. Choose a heading font and body font.
3. Type a name for the theme.
4. Click **Save**.

Managing custom themes and style sets

Exam Objective: MOS Word Core 1.3.3

Word groups themes into Style Sets, which provide a convenient way to format your documents' elements at one go. You can save, load, or reset themes by using the commands at the bottom of the Themes and Style Sets galleries.

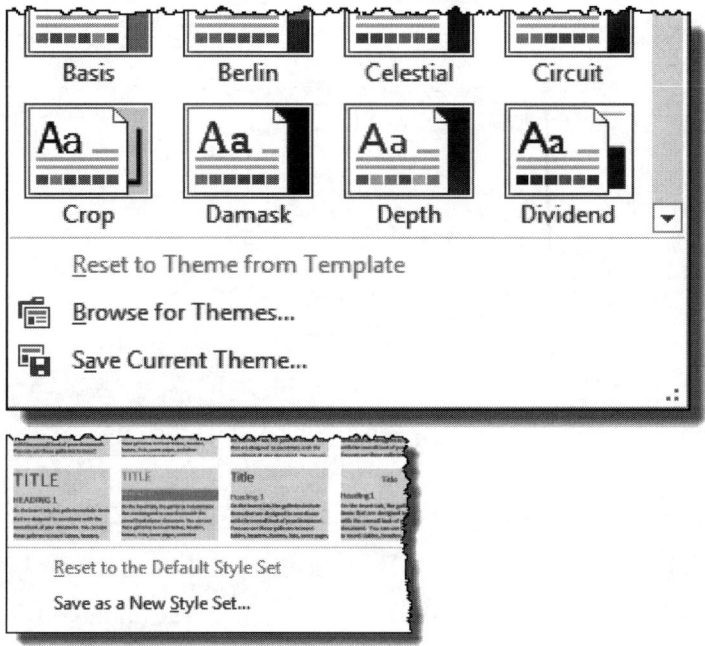

Exam Objective: MOS Word Expert 4.2.3, 4.2.4

The Themes gallery contains commands specific to the themes themselves.

- Click **Themes > Save Current Theme** to save your current customizations for other documents. Themes by default are stored in the `Templates\Document Themes` folder.
- Click **Browse for Themes** to load a new theme file from elsewhere on your computer.
- Click **Reset to Theme from Template** to return to the theme specified in the document template.
- At the right of the Style Sets gallery, click the down arrow to open the gallery. Click **Reset to the Default Style Set** to return to default settings.
- Click **Save as a New Style Set** to create a new style set using the themes you've applied.

Exercise: Creating a custom theme

In this exercise, you'll apply customized theme elements to a document, and then save them as a new theme.

Exam Objective: MOS Word Core 4.2.3 and Expert 1.3.2

Do This	How & Why
1. Open `Sales chart` and save it as `Regional sales chart`.	The file already includes theme colors, fonts, and effects in the chart. **Note:** Opening downloaded files in Office applications can result in the document being displayed in Protected mode. This can be overridden by clicking **Enable Editing** at the top of the document window.
2. Customize the theme.	First, you'll change each element of the theme independently.
a) On the Design tab, in the Document Formatting group, click **Colors**.	To open the gallery. There's a set of colors for each built-in theme.
b) Point to different color sets in the gallery.	The chart columns change to preview each set, as do the title text and the line beneath it.
c) Click **Slipstream**.	To set the colors.
d) Click **Fonts**.	Each set of fonts shows the name of each font in its own typeface.
e) Click **Arial Black**.	You can preview others first, if you like. It changes all the fonts in the document: the title, the following paragraph, and the chart labels.
f) Click **Effects > Glossy**.	The outlines and shading on the chart columns are more distinct, to make up for the more subdued color scheme.
3. Create a new set of theme colors.	You'll alter the accent colors to make them stand out more clearly.
a) Click **Colors > Customize Colors**.	To open the Create New Theme Colors window.

Do This	How & Why
b) Click the color menu next to **Accent 2**.	 To see some available colors.
c) Click **More Colors**.	To open the Colors window. You'll pick a new one.
d) Click a light orange color, as shown.	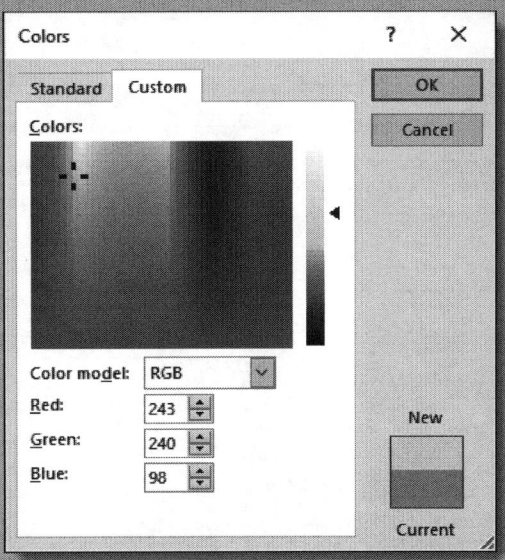
e) Click **OK**.	To return to the Create New Theme Colors window. Accent 2 is now the color you selected.
f) In the Name field, type `Tucana`.	
g) Click **Save**.	To apply the colors to the chart, and save them as a new theme color.
h) Click **Colors**.	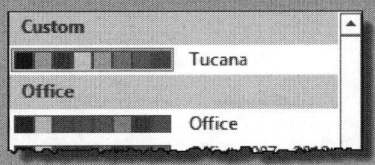 The Tucana color scheme now appears in the gallery.
i) Close the gallery.	
4. Save the customized theme.	You'll want to apply this theme to future sales reports, so you need to save it.
a) Click **Themes > Save Current Theme**.	You'll need to scroll to the bottom of the gallery. The Save Current Theme window opens. The Document Themes folder is selected.

Do This	How & Why
b) Name the file `Sales Chart`.	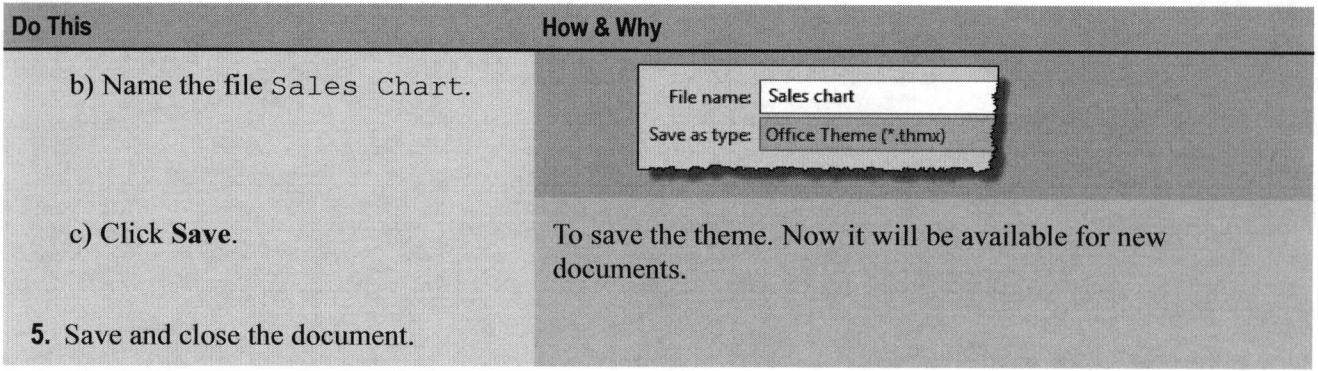
c) Click **Save**.	To save the theme. Now it will be available for new documents.
5. Save and close the document.	

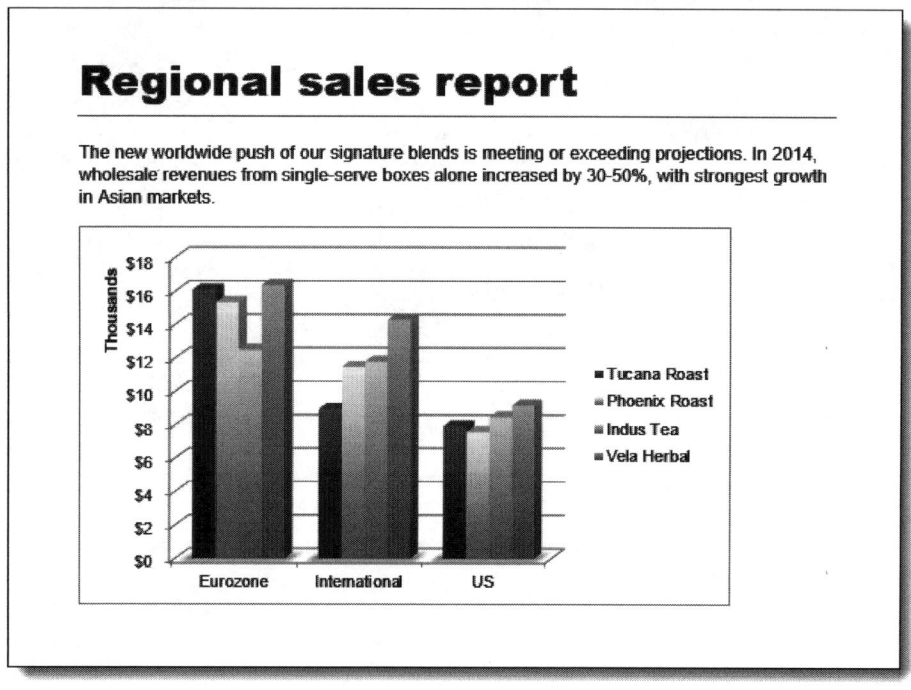

Assessment: Custom themes

Checking knowledge about theme customization.

1. What elements of a theme can you customize independently? Choose all that apply.

    - Colors
    - Effects
    - Fonts
    - Shapes
    - Styles

2. How many fonts can be defined in a theme? Choose the best answer.

    - 1
    - 2
    - 3
    - 4

3. When you change theme effects, doing so affects any graphical elements that use shape styles. True or false?

    - True
    - False

4. A Style Set can contain only a single theme. True or false?

    - True
    - False

Module B: Building blocks

Word includes a number of pre-formatted pieces of content, called building blocks, which you can insert into your documents. These include headers and footers, text boxes, cover pages, watermarks, and more.

You will learn:

- About building blocks
- How to insert building blocks
- How to insert Quick Parts

About building blocks

 Exam Objective: MOS Word Core 4.2.3

Most building blocks have a combination of formatting and graphics, as well as placeholder fields into which you can type your own text. You've probably used building blocks before when adding built-in headers and footers; others work mostly the same way. Building blocks don't generally do anything you can't do with manual formatting, but they make it quicker and easier to place and format content in your documents. Additionally, the built-in building blocks of different types have a number of matching formats. For example, you can use Puzzle footers, Puzzle sidebars, and a Puzzle cover page to give the whole document a consistent graphical style.

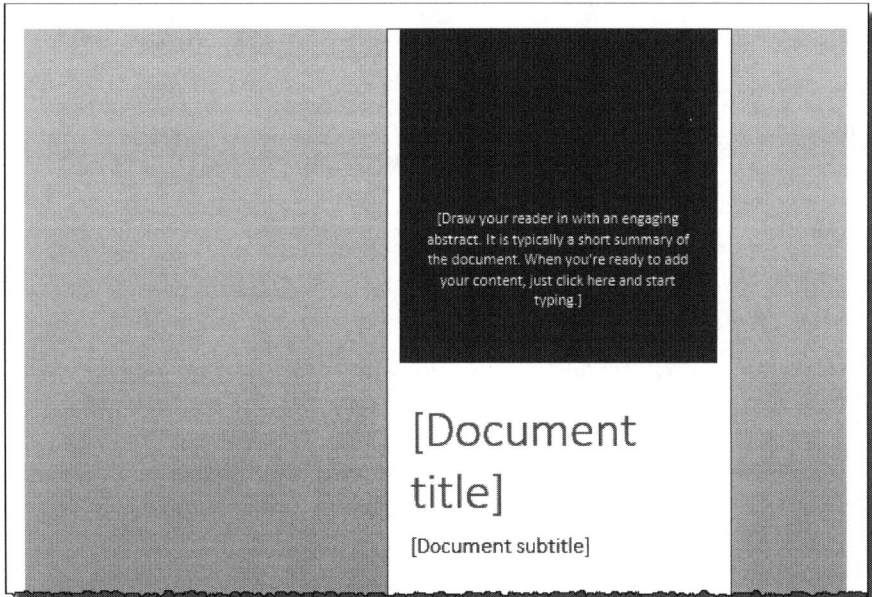

Inserting building blocks

Exam Objective: MOS Word Core 4.2.3

When you insert a building block, it is placed in an appropriate location for its type. For example, a header is placed at the top of every page, while a text box is inserted onto the current page, and you can move it if you like. Some building blocks are simply placed at the insertion point.

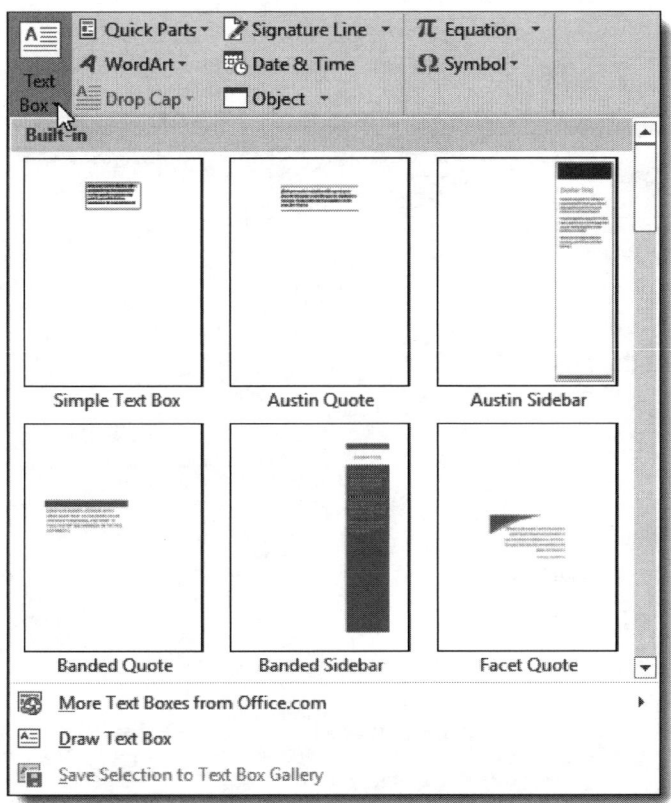

You can insert most building blocks by opening the gallery and clicking a selection, but some are a little more complex or are located inside other menus.

- The Insert tab contains most of the building-block galleries.
  - Click **Cover Page**, **Header**, **Footer**, or **Text Box** to open their respective galleries.
  - To view the Quick Tables gallery, click **Table > Quick Tables**.
  - To view the AutoText gallery, click **Quick Parts > AutoText**.
  - There are four Page Number galleries, grouped by where the number is located on the page: *Top of Page*, *Bottom of Page*, *Page Margins*, and *Current Position*. The first two appear in the header and footer areas, and replace any headers or footers you already have.
  - The Text Box gallery contains both quotes and sidebars. *Quotes* are small boxes meant to hold quotes or summaries from the main document, while *sidebars* are larger boxes meant to be placed on page edges and hold standalone supplements to the main document content. You can still move or use either however you like.
  - To open the Equations gallery, you must click the down arrow on the right of (or below) the ribbon command. Otherwise, you'll just insert a blank equation field.

- On the Design tab, click **Watermark** to open the watermark gallery.
- On the References tab, click **Table of Contents** or **Bibliography** to open its respective gallery.

Exercise: Inserting building blocks

In this exercise, you'll add built-in building blocks to a document.

Do This	How & Why
1. Open `Coffee houses`, and save it as `Building blocks`.	
2. Add page numbers to the document.	
a) On the Insert tab, click **Page Number**.	You can add page numbers in different areas of the page. Each has its own gallery.
b) Click **Bottom of Page**.	The gallery has several categories, each with its own set of page number styles.
c) Click **Thick Line**.	It's around the middle of the list. The page number is inserted under a thick line at the bottom of the page and the footer text is active.
d) Click **Close Header and Footer**.	On the Header & Footer Tools Design tab. You could also just double-click the main body text. Like a normal footer, it's applied to the entire document.
3. Add a quote box.	Instead of directly quoting, you'll add a brief summary of the first section.
a) On the first page, place the insertion point at the beginning of the fourth paragraph.	Beginning with "Another account."
b) On the Insert tab, click **Text Box > Austin Quote**.	A pull-quote-style formatted text box is inserted, along with placeholder text explaining how to use it.
c) In the text box, type `"The history of coffee houses, ere the invention of clubs, was that of the manners, the morals and the politics of a people."`	You can cut and paste from the second paragraph.

Do This	How & Why
4. Insert a cover page.	You'll use the Austin cover page, to match the text boxes.
a) On the Insert tab, in the Pages group, click **Cover Page > Austin**.	The cover page is inserted at the beginning of the document. It has placeholder fields for Abstract, Title, Subtitle, and Author.
b) In the Title field, type `The Coffee Houses of Old London.`	
c) In the Subtitle field, type `From All About Coffee.`	
d) Select the text box containing the Author field.	It shows the Author field from the document's properties. It's not what you want here.
e) Press **Delete**.	
f) In the Abstract field, type `From William H. Ukers' All About Coffee, 1922. All content is public domain.`	
5. Save and close the document.	

Assessment: Building Blocks

1. You can best add page numbers using the Header or Footer galleries. True or false?

    - True
    - False

2. Which ribbon tab has most of the building block galleries? Choose the best answer.

    - Home
    - Insert
    - Design
    - References

3. Before inserting a building block, you always need to place the insertion point where you want it to go. For example, before adding a header building block, you should edit the header. True or false?

    - True
    - False

Module C: Section breaks

Normally, page layout options such as margins, columns, and page numbers affect the whole document. Very often, that's just how you want it, but when you need to, you can instead break your document into sections, and change page layout for each section independently.

You will learn:

- About section breaks
- How to change layout options for individual sections
- How to change page numbers for individual sections
- How to use headers and footers in multi-section documents

About section breaks

 Exam Objective: MOS Word Core 2.3.2, 2.3.3

When you break a document into sections, each section can have its own layout options. Not all layout features can be applied section by section, but many can. These include:

- Paper size
- Page orientation
- Margins
- Columns
- Headers and Footers
- Page and line numbering

A section break can be continuous (the next section begins on the same page) or can include a page break. A section break isn't obvious when printing—only its effects are. When you display formatting symbols, a section break appears as a double dotted line labeled "Section Break (Type)."

Two section breaks in a document, one Next Page and one Continuous.

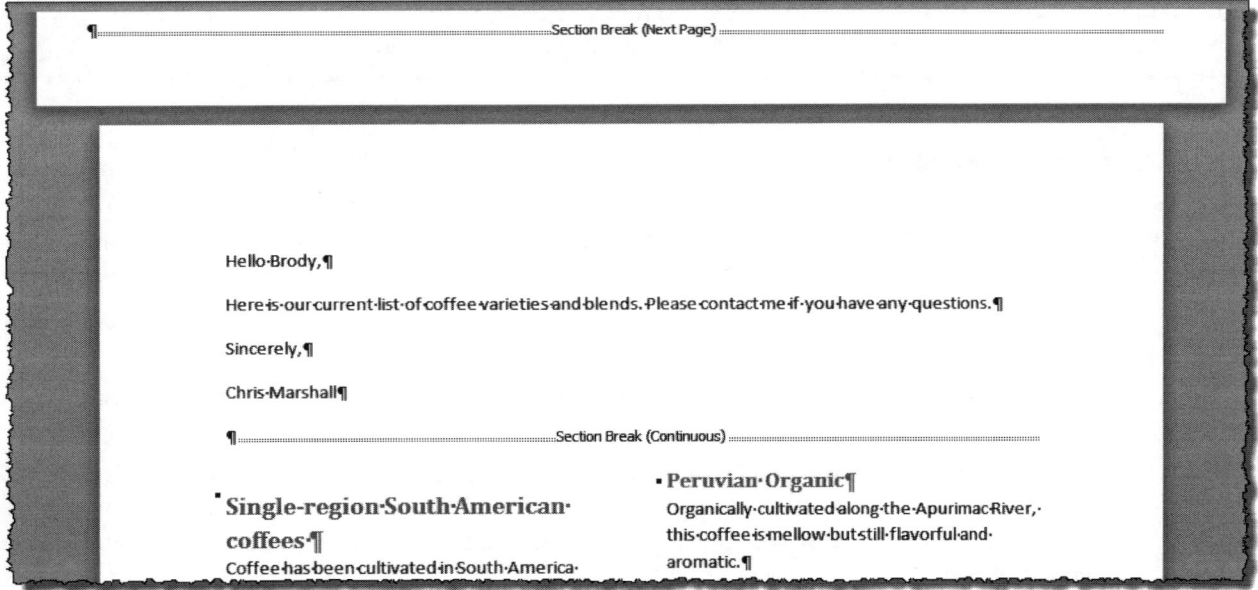

Inserting section breaks

To insert section breaks, click **Breaks** on the Page Layout tab and pick a type. Which type you should choose depends on what you plan to do with the new section.

   Exam Objective: MOS Word Core 2.3.2

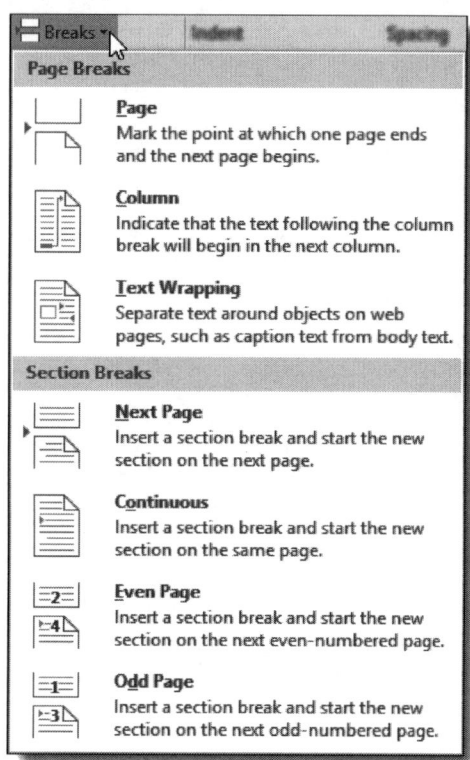

- To begin the new section on the next page, click **Breaks > Next Page**. This is best when you want to change something like page numbers, headers and footers, or page orientation.

- To start a new section on the same page, click **Breaks > Continuous**. This is best if you want to change something like columns or margins without otherwise disrupting the flow of the text.

- To start a new section on the next even-numbered page—inserting a new blank page, if necessary—click **Breaks > Even Page**.

- To start a new section on the next odd-numbered page, click **Breaks > Odd Page**. This is useful if you want each chapter of a document to begin on an odd-numbered (right-side) page.

Formatting document sections

Once you've inserted section breaks, most layout changes affect only the current section by default. If you want to apply the same change to more than one section, you can apply it individually to each. Depending on the type of change, you might be able to apply it to multiple sections at once, or even to the entire document.

   Exam Objective: MOS Word Core 2.3.3

- When formatting symbols are displayed, you can cut, paste, or delete a section break as you would any other content.

     Note: Word stores all formatting information for a section in the section break at its end. This means that if you delete a section break, the formatting of the *previous* section will be removed. It also means that if you move or copy a section break, its properties will apply to the section above its new location.

- To apply any compatible formatting to a single section, click within the section, and apply the formatting as you would to a normal document.
- You can apply changes in margins, paper size, or page orientation to multiple sections from the appropriate tab of the **Page Setup** window. To open it, click the launcher button in the Page Setup group.

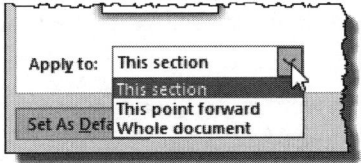

  - Choose **This Section** to apply only to the current section.
  - Choose **Whole document** to apply to all sections in the document.
  - Choose **This point forward** to apply to the current section and all following sections.
- To change a section break from one type to another, click in the following section and open the Page Setup window. Choose an option from the Section Start list on the Layout tab.

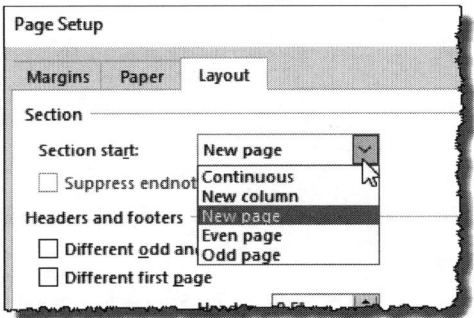

- In addition to changing page number formats for each section, you can also have a section's page numbers begin wherever you like. This is useful if you want each chapter of a document to have its own formatting. In the Insert tab's Header & Footer group, click **Page Number > Format Page Numbers**, and then select the desired options in the Page Number Format window.

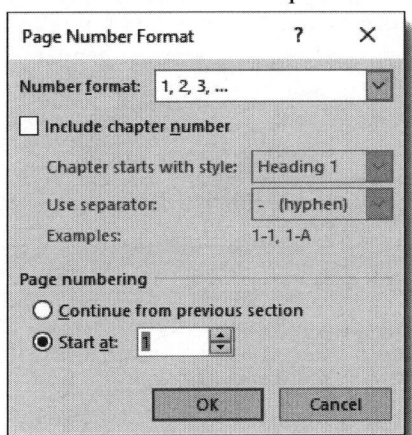

- A section break is often used as to signal a major division in a document. Thus, each section often has its own heading or title, signaling an important demarcation point to the reader. When working with section breaks, it's important to remember that any added section title should be placed *after* the break, not before it. This ensures that the title appears at the beginning of the new section.
- Each section can be formatted in significantly different ways. For example, a section could be formatted entirely in a multi-column format by using the **Page Layout > Columns** command.

Linked headers and footers

When you apply a header or footer to a document with multiple sections, it appears to apply to the whole document. This isn't because you can't apply it to one section at a time, but instead because by default each header and footer is linked to that of the previous section, and it to the one before that, back to the beginning of the document. Don't confuse this with other kinds of "linking" in Word: it simply means that all the linked headers or footers are identical, and changing one changes all of them.

You can tell if a header or footer is linked just by looking at it while it's selected: On the left side, it shows the section number, and if it's linked, the right side displays the label "Same as Previous."

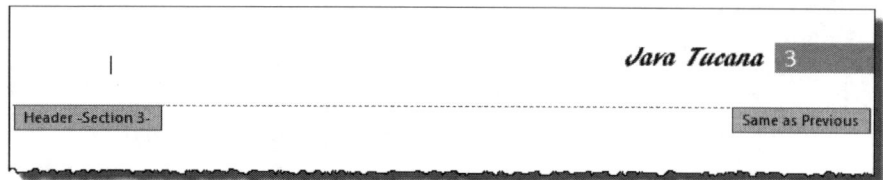

You can also look at the Header & Footer Tools Design tab, in the Navigation group. If the section is linked, the Link to Previous button is highlighted.

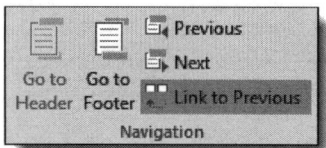

Because headers and footers are linked by default, it's easy to use one set through the entire document, no matter how many sections you make.

Managing section headers and footers

Linking and unlinking section headers or footers is simple in itself, but it can be confusing and frustrating if you don't keep in mind how the process works. The most important thing to remember is that links are always between the current section's header or footer and that of the previous section. If you're just going to unlink them all and set them individually, that's not a problem, but if you want to have an identical header in some sections but not others, you'll have to think carefully about the order in which you edit them.

 Exam Objective: MOS Word Core 2.3.3

For example, if you want sections 1 and 3 to have one header and section 2 to have a different one, you'll have to break the link for both section 2 and the one for section 3. It might be quickest for you to set the header for 1 and 3, then break the links, and finally change the header for 2.

For another example, imagine that you have a document with nine sections, and you break the header link between section 4 and section 3. This now means you have two headers, each for a different series of sections. If you were to change the header for section 2, it would affect sections 1–3, while if you changed the header for section 7, it would change sections 4–9. When you change a header for one section, always keep in mind what other sections might be changed.

If the current header or footer is unlinked, and you link it again, you're prompted to confirm the link. This is because it deletes the current section's header or footer, along with that of any following sections, and replaces it with the previous one. If you've spent a lot of time carefully formatting the current header or footer, this can cost you work.

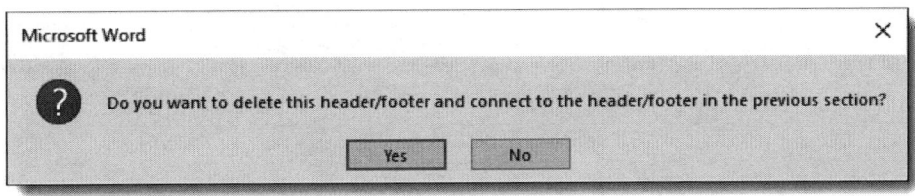

Finally, remember that headers and footers are linked or unlinked independently. Even if you use a different header for each section, you can have a linked footer for the whole document, and vice-versa.

1. Double-click the header or footer you want to edit.
2. On the Design tab, in the Navigation group, use the **Previous** and **Next** buttons to find the section you want to link or unlink.
3. Click **Link to Previous** to link or unlink the current section's header/footer.

Exercise: Using section breaks

Demonstrating use of section breaks.

In this exercise, you'll use section breaks to format individual parts of a document.

Exam Objective: MOS Word Core 2.3.2, 2.3.3

Do This	How & Why
1. Open `Coffee houses`, and save it as `Coffee house sections`.	
2. Display formatting marks, if necessary.	On the Home tab, click ¶ or press **Ctrl+***.
3. Insert section breaks.	You want to have each first-level heading begin a new section, on a new page.
a) Place the insertion point right before "The First London Coffee House."	At the beginning of the line.
b) On the Layout tab, click **Breaks > Next Page**.	of the manners, the morals and the politics of a people." And so the London coffee houses of the seventeenth and eighteenth ce indeed the history of the manners and customs of the English pe period.¶ ....Section Break (Next Page)............
	The new section now starts on page 2.
c) Navigate to page 6.	The next Heading 1 text is "Strange coffee mixtures."
d) Insert a new section break before the heading.	Place the insertion point, then click **Breaks > Next Page**. The heading now begins the next page.
e) Insert Next Page section breaks for the remaining first-level headings.	First-level headings are in green text. You'll find them on pages 10, 12, and 13 as you move forward.
4. Change the column settings for one part of the document.	

Chapter 2: Managing documents / Module C: Section breaks

Do This	How & Why
a) Place the insertion point at the beginning of the poem on page 3.	You'll format these verses to appear in two columns on the page.
b) Click **Columns > Two**.	The change applies to the whole section. That isn't what you want.
c) Press **Ctrl+Z**.	To undo the change. You'll make the poem its own section.
d) Click **Breaks > Continuous**.	To insert a section break without a page break.
e) Insert a continuous section break at the end of the poem.	Place the insertion point at the beginning of the second paragraph on page 4, then insert the break.
f) Place the insertion point in the poem, and click **Columns > Two**.	This time the formatting applies only to the poem itself.
5. Add a header and footer to the document.	
a) On the Insert tab, click **Header > Austin**.	This header has a field for the document title.
b) In the title field, type `The Coffee Houses of Old London`.	
c) Insert the Austin footer.	On the Insert tab, click **Footer > Austin**. This footer just has a page number, so you don't need to edit anything.
d) On the Design tab, click **Close Header & Footer**.	Or double-click the document body.

Do This	How & Why
6. Scroll through the document.	Because headers and footers are linked, the same set was applied to all sections of the document.
7. Remove the header from the first section.	If you just removed it directly, it would affect the entire document.
a) Double-click the header.	

The section number you see depends on how far down you scrolled.

[Header screenshot showing "The Coffee Houses of Old London", "Header -Section 3-", "The Vertue of the COFFEE Drink", "Concerning London's second coffee-house keeper, James Farr, proprietor of the Rainbow", "Same as Previous"]

The section number is shown on the left. The right shows that it's linked to the previous section.

Do This	How & Why
b) On the Design tab, in the Navigation group, click **Previous**.	[Previous button] To move to the previous section. It's also linked.
c) Navigate to Section 2.	Keep clicking **Previous** until it displays Section 2.
d) Click **Link to Previous**.	[Link to Previous button] To deselect it. The "Same as Previous" marker vanishes.
e) Navigate to Section 1's header.	Removing the link didn't change the header, but now you can edit it without affecting the other sections. You'll remove the title text but keep the border.
f) Delete the Title field.	Select the whole field, and press **Delete**. You might have to click in the text to make the frame appear.
8. Scroll to the bottom of page 2.	Section 2's Footer is still linked, but that's how you want it.
9. Click **Close Header & Footer**.	The title still appears in the header starting on page 2. Page 1 shows only the page number at the bottom.
10. Save and close the document.	

Assessment: Section breaks

Checking knowledge about section breaks.

1. You want a full-page graphic in the middle of your document to print in landscape format. What's the best thing to do before changing the page orientation?

    - Insert a Next Page section break before the graphic.
    - Insert a Next Page section break after the graphic.
    - Insert Next Page section breaks before and after the graphic.
    - Insert Continuous section breaks before and after the graphic.

2. There are two sections in your document: the first has two columns, and the second has one column. If you delete the section break between them, what happens? Choose the best answer.

    - The whole document will have one column.
    - The whole document will have two columns.
    - It depends whether it was a New Page or Continuous break.

3. You can change margins, paper size, or page orientation for multiple sections at a time. True or false?

    - True
    - False

4. After creating 8 sections in a document, you unlink section 4's footer and then edit it. What parts of the document are changed?

    - The headers and footers for sections 1–4.
    - The headers and footers for sections 4–8.
    - The footers for sections 1–4.
    - The footers for sections 4–8.
    - Only section 4's footer.

Module D: Page backgrounds

In addition to placing content on the pages of your document, you can also place it on the *page background*, as though your document were printed on colored or patterned paper. You can thus format the pages of your documents with watermarks, colors, textures, or borders.

You will learn how to:

- Apply watermarks
- Set background colors and patterns
- Set page borders

About page backgrounds

There are three types of page background options. All three are found on the Design tab in the Page Background group, but each has a distinct function, and Word handles each in a different way.

 Exam Objective: MOS Word Core 1.3.6

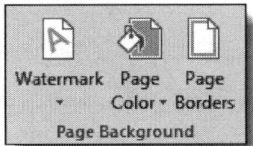

Watermark	An image or text, usually transparent, centered on the page. Watermarks are generally functional, showing where the document comes from or how it's meant to be used. For example, you might insert your company logo as a watermark, or you might place a "CONFIDENTIAL" watermark on a document you don't want freely distributed.
Page Color	A background across the entire page, usually just to enhance the document's appearance. It can be a solid color, as the name implies, but can also be a gradient, texture, or picture of your choice.
Page borders	A border placed around the entire page, just like one around a paragraph or table cell. It can simply be a line, or one of a variety of built-in artistic effects.

You can add any combination of page backgrounds you want, but only one of each type.

Creating custom watermarks

The Watermark gallery contains several predefined options that you can insert as you would any other building block, but you can also create a custom watermark.

 Exam Objective: MOS Word Core 1.3.6

1. On the Design tab, click **Watermark > Custom Watermark** to open the Printed Watermark window.
2. Click **Picture Watermark** or **Text watermark**.
3. Set watermark options.
   - For a picture watermark, click **Select Picture** to choose an image file from your computer.
   - For a text watermark, choose one of the text options, or type your own. You can also choose the language, font, and color, and whether to place the watermark horizontally or diagonally on the page.
   - By default, watermarks are automatically sized to fit the page. To override this setting, choose an option from the Scale or Size field, depending on the watermark type.
   - By default, watermarks are transparent, so that they don't make the document text hard to read. To override this, clear **Washout** or **Semitransparent**, as available.
4. Click **OK**.

Setting page colors and fills

Setting a solid page color is like coloring any other element: click **Page Color**, and choose the color you want. Click **Fill Effects** to set more advanced options from the Fill Effects window. The available options vary for each type of effect.

 Exam Objective: MOS Word Core 1.3.6

- Gradient effects cover the page in a smooth color transition.
  - The gradient can contain two colors of your choice, one color plus a grayscale value, or a set of predefined colors.
  - You can choose the direction of the gradient by clicking one value from the Shading styles list, and one from the Variants list.

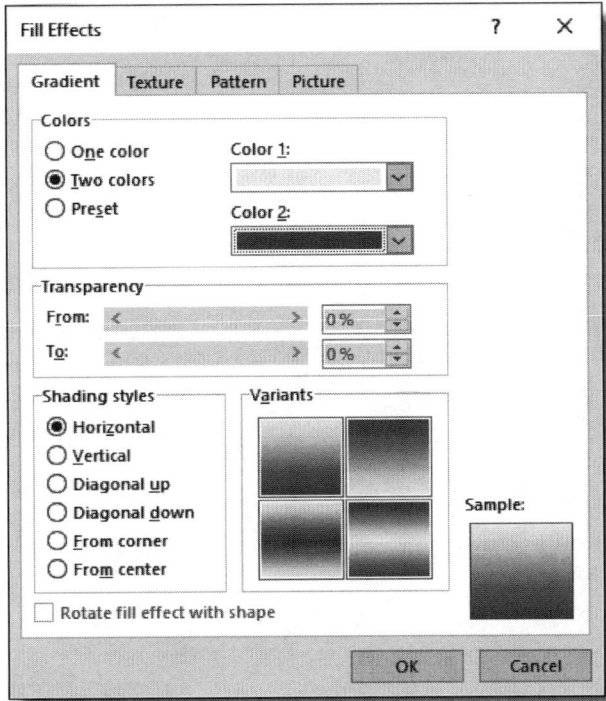
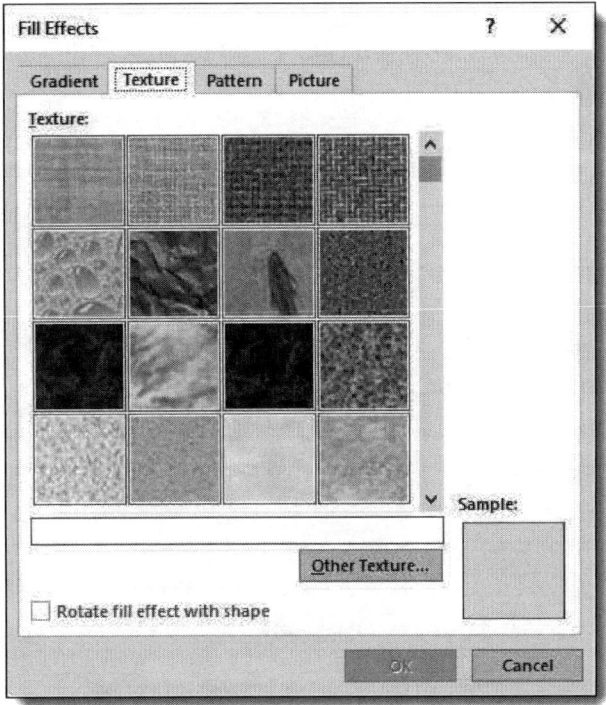
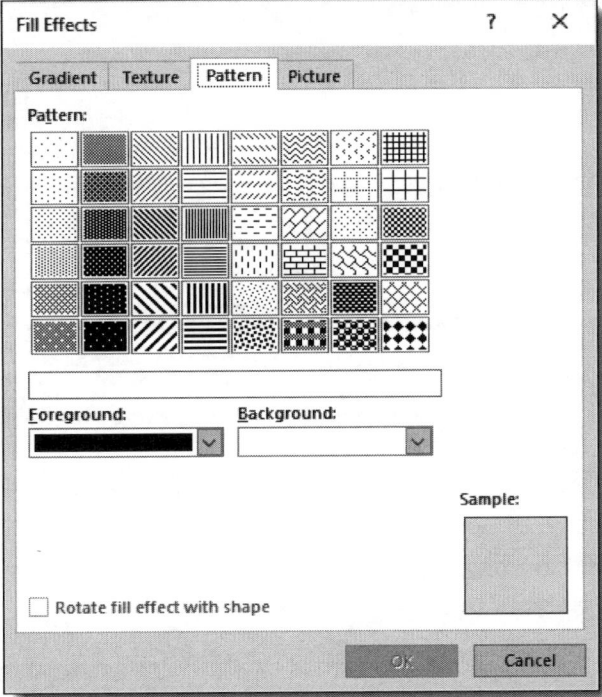

- Texture effects smoothly tile a small image over the whole page. You can choose a predefined texture or insert an image of your own.
- Pattern effects tile a simple graphical pattern over the page. You can select only from predefined patterns, but you can set the foreground and background colors for each.
- Picture effects place an image file of your choice across the page. Pictures tile like textures, but are intended more for a single, large image across the page.

Page colors and fills are generally intended to add graphical interest to a digital document. On paper, they can waste ink or make the document hard to read, so by default Word won't print them. To change this setting, check **Print background colors and images** in the Display section of the Word Options window.

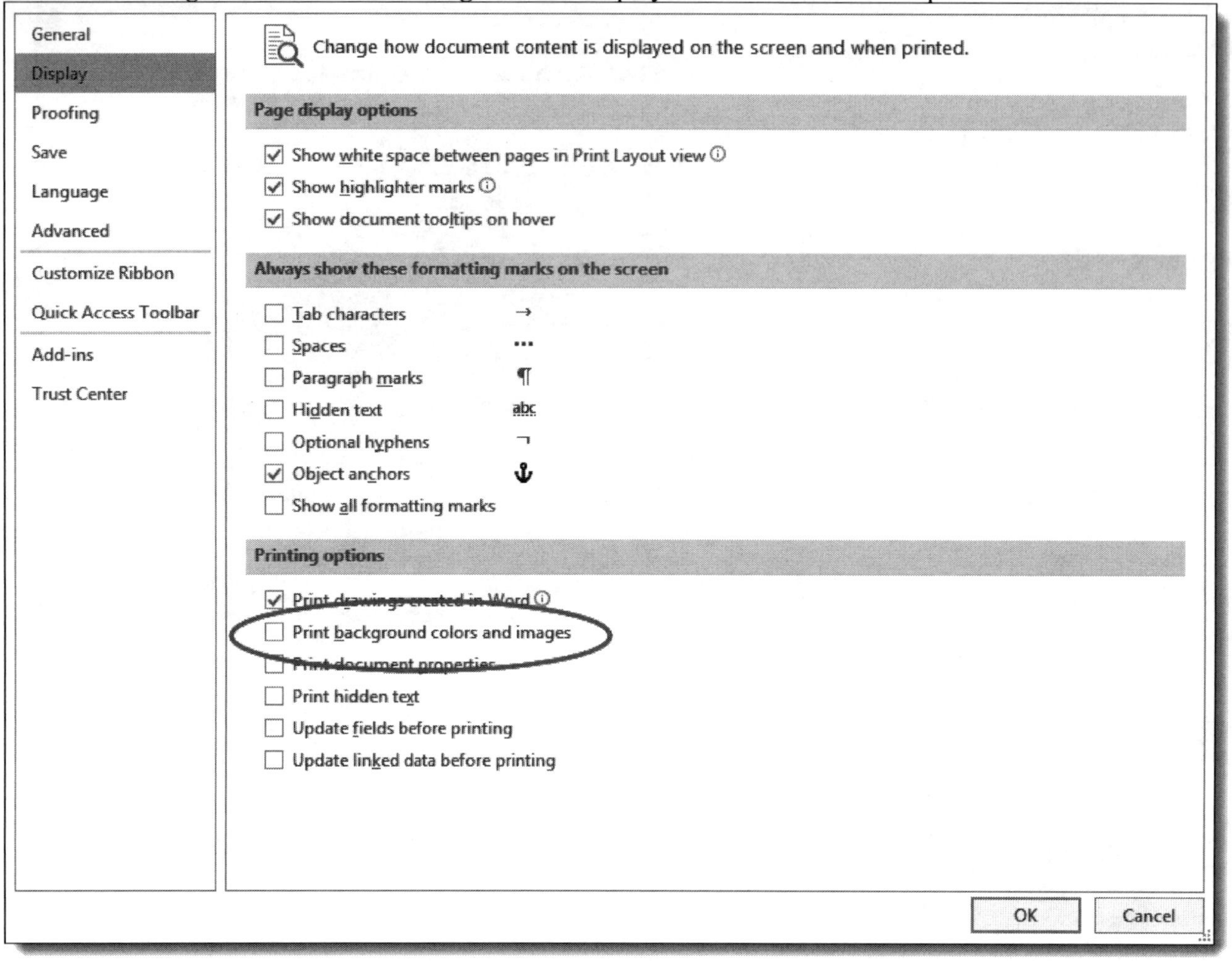

Setting page borders

You can define a page border from the Design tab, in the Page Background group, by clicking **Page Borders**, then setting options in the Borders and Shading window.

 Exam Objective: MOS Word Core 1.3.6

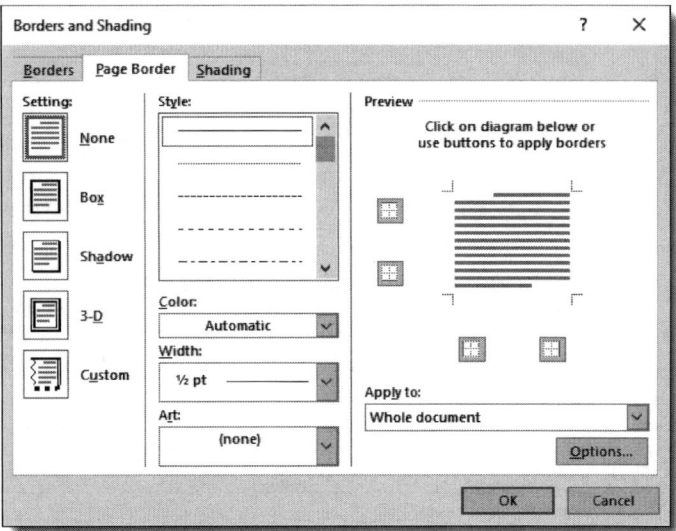

If you've set other borders in Word, you can set page borders, as they aren't much different. There are multiple kinds of options you can configure, but not all combinations are compatible.

- Choose the overall effect of the border from the Setting section. It can be a simple box, a box with a drop shadow, a 3-D effect, or a custom design.
- Click the buttons in the Preview section to display or remove individual sides of the border. This changes the Setting option to **Custom**, if it isn't already.
- Choose either a line style from the Style list, or a clip-art border from the Art list.
  - The Width field affects the thickness of both line and art borders. In general, clip-art borders should be thicker.
  - You can set a color for any line border, and for some—but not all—image borders.
- Choose what pages you want the border to appear on from the "Apply to" list. You can apply a border to the whole document, the current section, the first page, or everything but the first page.
- Click **Options** to choose position and display options in the Border and Shading Options window.

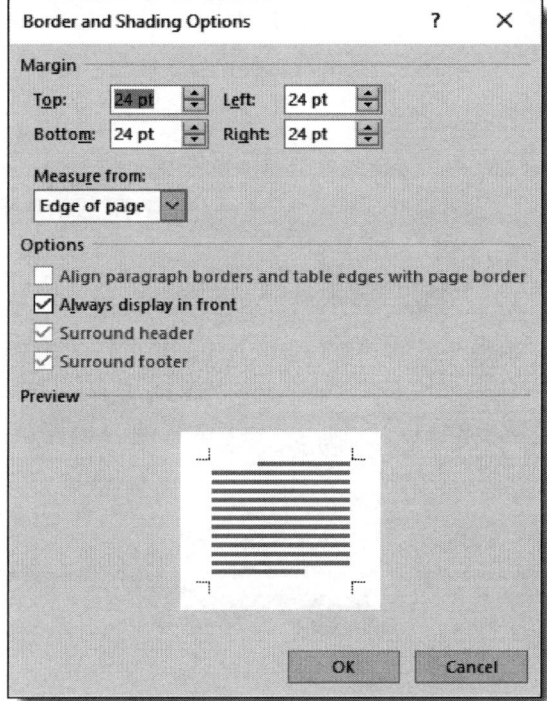

Page backgrounds and sections

When you use page backgrounds in documents with multiple sections, you might notice inconsistent behavior. This is because each of the three types of page background interacts differently with sections.

- As you just saw, page borders can be applied to the current section or the whole document from the Borders and Shading window.

- Any page color option applies to the entire document, regardless of whether you use sections or not. If you want to color just part of a document, you need to use another method, such as a shape placed behind the text.

- Watermarks function a little less intuitively in Word. Watermarks are tied to the document header and share the same linking structure. By default, this means it applies to the whole document, but if you want to watermark individual sections, you first need to unlink their headers.

Exercise: Setting a page background

In this exercise, you'll set a page color, page border, and watermark on a document.

Exam Objective: MOS Word Core 1.3.6

Do This	How & Why
1. Open `Lunch Menu`, and save it as `Lunch Menu background`.	
2. Add a page background.	The print menu in the café uses colored, textured paper, so you want the digital version to look similar.
a) On the Design tab, click **Page Color > Fill Effects**.	To open the Fill Effects window.
b) Click the **Texture** tab.	It shows a selection of image textures. You'll use one of these.
c) Click the **Parchment** texture, as shown.	
d) Click **OK**.	The background is applied to the page.
3. Add a page border.	
a) Click **Page Borders**.	The Borders and Shading window opens, with the Page Border tab active.

Do This	How & Why
b) Click the border style shown.	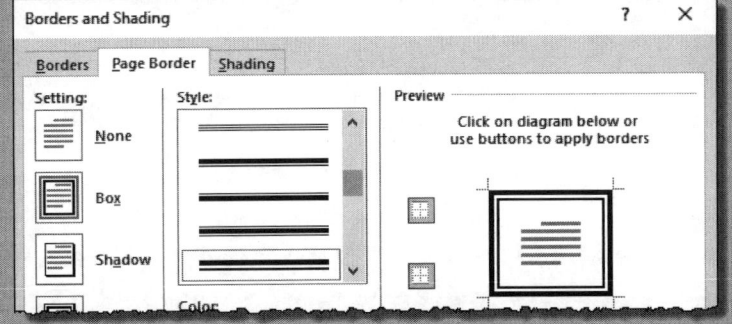
	It's about halfway down the list. Notice that it's reflected in the preview, and the Box setting is automatically selected as well.
c) In the Color list, click **Red, Accent 2, Darker 25%**.	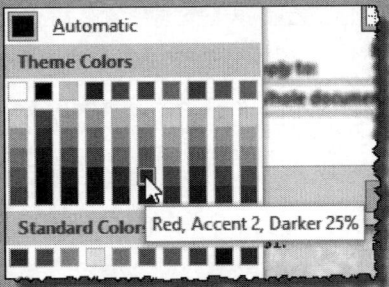
d) Click **OK**.	The border appears around the whole page.
4. Add a watermark.	This is still just a draft version, so you don't want any potential customers to think the menu and prices are final.
a) Click **Watermark > Draft 1**.	Scroll down to the Disclaimers section of the menu. A building-block watermark appears. It doesn't show up very well against the current page color, so you'll customize it.
b) Click **Watermark > Custom Watermark**.	To open the Printed Watermark window. Text Watermark is already selected, with the current settings.
c) From the Color list, click **Red, Accent 2**.	You'll leave the other settings the same.
d) Click **OK**.	The new color makes it stand out more, and because it's semitransparent, even similarly colored text is easy to read over it.
5. Save and close the document.	See the example on the next page.

Assessment: Page backgrounds

Checking knowledge about page backgrounds.

1. You can apply multiple watermarks to a single page. True or false?

    - True
    - False

2. What fill effect would you use to cover the page in a smooth color transition? Choose the best response.

    - Gradient
    - Pattern
    - Picture
    - Texture

3. If you like, you can create a page border that appears only on the left and right of the page. True or false?

    - True
    - False

4. How can you apply a watermark to a single section?

    - Choose "This Section" from the "Apply to" list when you create it.
    - Make sure the section's header is unlinked from the other sections.
    - You can apply a watermark only to the entire document.

Summary: Managing documents

You should now know how to:

- Create custom themes by separately choosing fonts, themes, and effects
- Quickly insert pre-formatted document content using building blocks
- Vary page layout throughout a document by separating it into sections
- Apply page backgrounds behind the text of a document

Synthesis: Managing documents

Bringing together your knowledge of document management.

In this exercise, you'll format a large document with page layout and reusable content tools.

1. Open **Coffee houses**, and save it as `Coffee houses synthesis`.

     Note: Because you'll be doing similar work, you might want to start with `Coffee House Sections` instead.

2. Improve the document's layout on a section-by-section basis.
    - Each page after the first should have a header corresponding to a first-level heading.
    - All quoted poetry should be displayed either in two columns or using wider margins, depending on which fits better.

3. Customize the document's appearance to make it more visually appealing.
    - Create a custom theme using a mix of colors, fonts, and effects.
    - Insert a cover page, header and footer, text boxes, and other building blocks. Coordinate your choices with your theme decision.
    - Choose a page color and border to match the rest of your customizations.

4. Save and close the document.

Chapter 3: Styles

You will learn how to:

- Create and modify character styles for applying combinations of formatting to characters, words, and phrases.
- Create and modify paragraph styles for applying formatting to paragraphs as a whole

Module A: Character styles

You will learn how to:

- Use advanced character formatting attributes.
- Create and modify character styles.
- Use paste options to copy only certain attributes of text.

Advanced character formatting

Most common font controls are located on the ribbon, but you can access the rest from the Font window. In addition to providing the same controls found in the Font group, the Font window gives you additional control over font attributes, effects, character spacing, and advanced features used in OpenType fonts.

Exam Objective: MOS Word Core 2.1.1

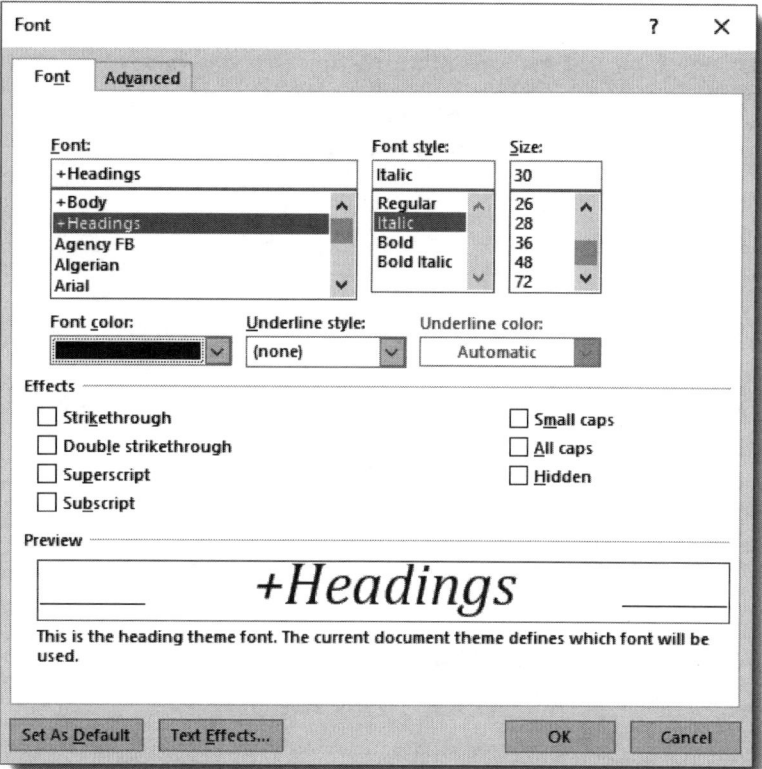

At the bottom of the window, a preview shows the result of the selected attributes.

Setting font attributes

Exam Objective: MOS Word Core 4.3.4 and Expert 2.2.1

To open the Font window, click the **Launcher** button in the Font group. Most of the controls correspond or add directly to those on the ribbon, but there are other useful ones.

- The +Body and +Headings fonts correspond to the Theme fonts on the ribbon, and change whenever the document's theme does. Other fonts override theme settings.

- Clicking **Text Effects** at the bottom of the window opens the Format Text Effects window, which provides more detailed settings than the Text Effects menu on the ribbon.
- The Character Spacing section on the Advanced tab lets you stretch or compress text horizontally, adjust its spacing, and shift its vertical position.
- If you're using newer OpenType fonts, the OpenType Features section lets you set options for ligatures, number spacing, number forms, and stylistic sets.

Using nonbreaking spaces

One very useful special symbol is the *nonbreaking space*. Sometimes, you want a two- or several-word phrase to stay together on line, without breaking across an automatic line break. This might be true for a product name, for example. There are a couple of ways to insert a non-breaking space.

- On the Insert tab, click **Symbol > More Symbols**. Click the Special Characters tab, click **Nonbreaking space**, and then click **Insert**.
- Hold **Ctrl+Shift**, and press the spacebar.
    If you have symbols showing in your document, the nonbreaking space will look slightly different than a normal space.

① Normal space.

② Nonbreaking space.

Exercise: Applying advanced character attributes

In this exercise, you'll apply character attributes using the Font window.

Do This	How & Why
1. Open `JT-Coffee` and save it as `JT-Coffee-formatting`.	In the data location for the chapter. **Note:** Opening downloaded files in Office applications can result in the document's being displayed in Protected View. This can be overridden by clicking **Enable Editing** at the top of the document window.
2. In the Phoenix Roast section, select "Columbian Bogota."	You'll format coffee names inside paragraph text so they stand out.
3. Set font attributes for the text.	
a) In the Font group, click 🔻	You can instead press **Ctrl+D**. The Font window opens.

Do This	How & Why
b) From the Font color list, choose the following color.	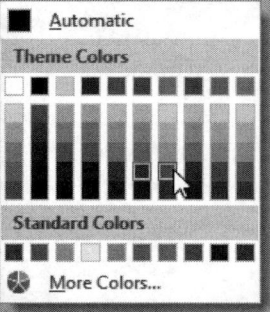 Olive Green, Accent 3, Darker 25%.
c) From the Underline style list, choose the first line option.	
d) From the Underline color list, choose **Orange, Accent 6**.	The top color in the last column.  The results are displayed in the Preview section, so it doesn't matter whether you can see the page.
4. Adjust the character spacing.	Switch to the Advanced tab.
a) From the Spacing list, select **Condensed**.	Under Character Spacing. In the preview, the letters grow closer together.
b) From the Scale list, select **150%**.	The letters are stretched out horizontally. You'll reduce the effect a bit.
c) In the scale list, type `120%`	You can enter your own values as well as select them.
d) Press **Tab**.	The text is now only a little wider than before, but with broader letters. 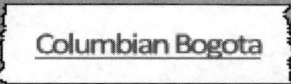
5. Click **OK**.	The formatting is now applied to the text.
6. How could you format the other coffee names the same way?	Doing it all manually would be slow. You could do it fairly quickly by using the Format Painter. But you're going to see a better way: using a character style.
7. Observe the Costa Rican Tarrazu product name.	It breaks across a line break. You will use nonbreaking spaces to prevent this.

Do This	How & Why
8. Insert nonbreaking spaces in the Costa Rican Tarrazu product name.	
a) Select the space between "Costa" and "Rican".	
b) While holding **Ctrl+Shift**, press the spacebar.	To insert a non-breaking space in the product name. Now, the first two words stay together, moving to the next line in the document.
c) Insert a non-breaking space between "Rican" and "Tarrazu".	Select the space between he words, hold **Ctrl+Shift**, then press the spacebar.
9. Save the file.	Do not close it.

Custom styles

For a novice user, it's easy to see the Styles gallery as a convenient box of pre-defined formatting options, and font and paragraph controls as something to use when there isn't a style with the right look. When you're making simple documents, this approach is fine, but the real strength of styles is how you can modify them throughout the entire document, or create entirely new ones for formats you use often.

For example, by default the Strong style looks exactly like bold text, so you might wonder why you need the style at all. But suppose that later on you decide you want to make all the bold text red or set it in a different font. If you were to use the Strong style, you could change it all at once by modifying the style, but if you were simply to use the Bold button, you would have to select and reformat every occurrence of bold text all over again throughout the document.

There are three types of styles: character, paragraph, and linked. Which you use depends on what you want to do with them.

 Exam Objective: MOS Word Expert 2.2.1, 2.2.2

- *Character styles* contain only font formatting elements, not paragraph formatting elements. This means you can apply them to any amount of text, from a single character to an entire message.

- *Paragraph styles* can contain both font formatting elements and paragraph formatting elements. You can apply a paragraph style only to entire paragraphs, not to part of one.

- *Linked styles* can also contain both font and paragraph formatting elements, but can behave as either character or paragraph styles, depending on how you apply them. If you apply a linked style to an entire paragraph, it has the effect of a paragraph style, but if you apply it to part of a paragraph, only its character elements are applied.

Using a custom character style to format text

Tucana Roast
Our signature roast blends Brazilian Bourbon Santos with Guatemalan Coban. The re[...] is remarkably rich and fragrant yet clean, sweet, and snappy. The perfect cup for aft[...]

Creating character styles by example

 Exam Objective: MOS Word Expert 2.2.1

You can create new styles from either the Styles gallery or the Styles pane. In either case, the style is initially based on whatever text you have selected, so you might want to start by formatting or selecting text to match somewhat the style you want to make. The simplest way to create a style is by example; you just format the text as you want the style, then define a name for it.

1. Format text for which you want to create a style and select it.
   You don't have to do this, but it gives you a head start on defining the style.

2. In the bottom-right of the Styles group, click the Styles button.
   This is the Styles button.

   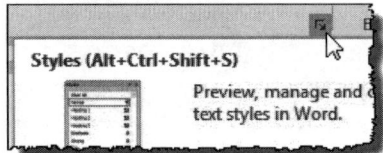

   The Styles pane appears on the right side of the window. You can use to the Style to create, apply, and modify styles.

   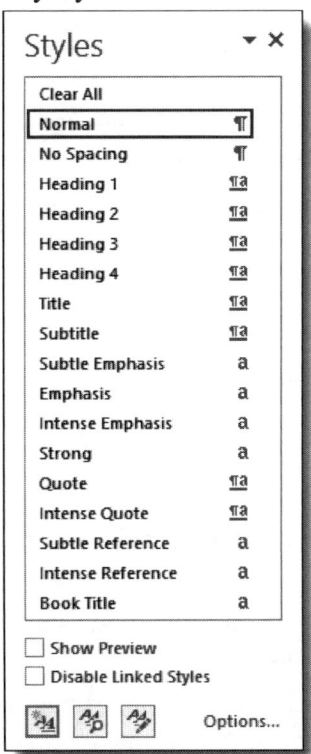

3. Click .
   The New Style button displays the Create New Style from Formatting window.

4. Type a name for your style.
   When you create a style in this way, it will be a linked style by default. You will need to modify the style to make it a character style.

5. Click **Modify**.
   To display the full Create New Style from Formatting window.

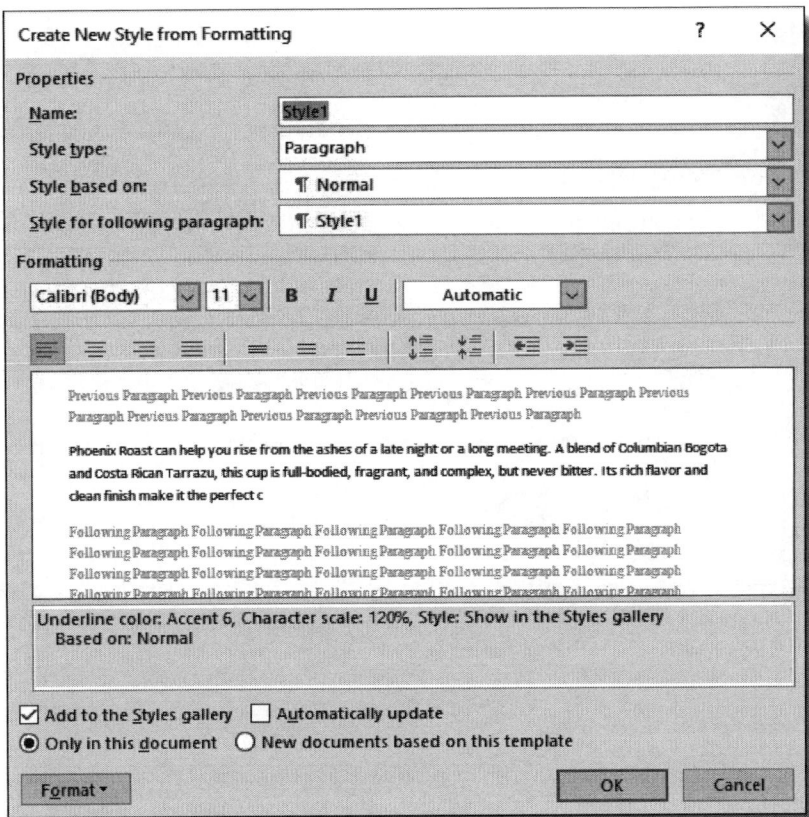

6. In the Name box, enter a name for the style.
7. In the Style Type list, click **Character**.

   This will make this a character style rather than a Paragraph style.
8. Click **OK**.

Defining a new character style

If you want to definite or modify style attributes while you create a style, you'll want to use the full Create New Style from Formatting window.

1. Format text for which you want to create a style and select it.
2. Display the Create New Style from Formatting window.
    In the Styles pane, click the New Style button.
3. Set the properties for the style.
    These include the name, the type, and what the style is based on.
4. Define formatting for the style.
    - Use the formatting toolbar in the window to apply simple formatting like font, bold, and italic.

    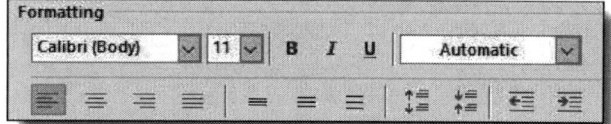

    - Click the **Format** button, then an option to display deeper formatting options.

    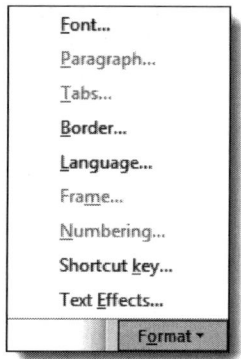

5. Click **OK**.

After creating a character style, you can easily apply to selected text by clicking the style name either in the Style gallery or in the Styles pane.

Exercise: Creating and applying character styles

For this exercise, you need to have `JT-Coffee-formatting` open, and to have completed the **Applying advanced character attributes** exercise. You'll create a character style for coffee names, then apply that style to other text in the document.

Exam Objective: MOS Word Expert 2.2.1

Do This	How & Why
1. Observe the coffee names within the document's paragraphs.	Only one ("Columbian Bogota") is formatted. You would like to create a character style so you can format all the similar text in the same way.
2. Select **Columbian Bogota**.	The formatted text under the Phoenix Roast heading.
3. Open the Styles pane.	Click the launcher button in the Styles group. The Styles pane appears to the right of the document. You can use the Styles pane to create, apply, and modify styles in your documents.
4. In the Styles pane, click .	The New Style button. The Create New Style from Formatting window opens.
5. In the Name box, enter `Product Name`.	To create a name for the new style you are are creating. This name will appear in both the Style gallery and Style pane.
6. Define this as a character style.	
a) Observe the Style type box.	The default type of style is Paragraph, but you want this to be a Character style.
b) In the Style type list, click **Character**.	
7. Observe the style's definition.	

Below the sample box. It shows all the formatting that has been applied to the style on which your style is based.

> Underline, Underline color: Accent 6, Font color: Accent 3, Condensed by 1 pt, Character scale: 120%, Style: Show in the Styles gallery, Priority: 2
>   Based on: Default Paragraph Font

Chapter 3: Styles / Module A: Character styles

Do This	How & Why
8. Observe the formatting options. • The toolbar in the window gives you quick access to simple formatting such as the font, its size, and bold or italic. • Click the **Format** button to display a menu of options you can click to display other formatting windows.	
9. Click **OK**.	To create the style, which now appears in the list in the Styles pane.
10. Apply the Product name style to other coffee names in the body text. a) In the same paragraph, select "Costa Rican Tarrazu."	
b) Click **Product Name**.	You can click it in the Styles pane or Styles gallery. Notice that there is a small "a" to the right of the style name in the Styles pane. This, as opposed to the paragraph symbol (¶) indicates that this is a character style. The text is now formatted to match the style.
c) Apply the Product name style to other coffees named as blend ingredients.	Brazilian Bourbon Santos and Guatemalan Coban in the Tucana Roast paragraph. You don't need to apply it when a coffee is referenced in its own description.
11. Save the file.	

Character styles applied to the document

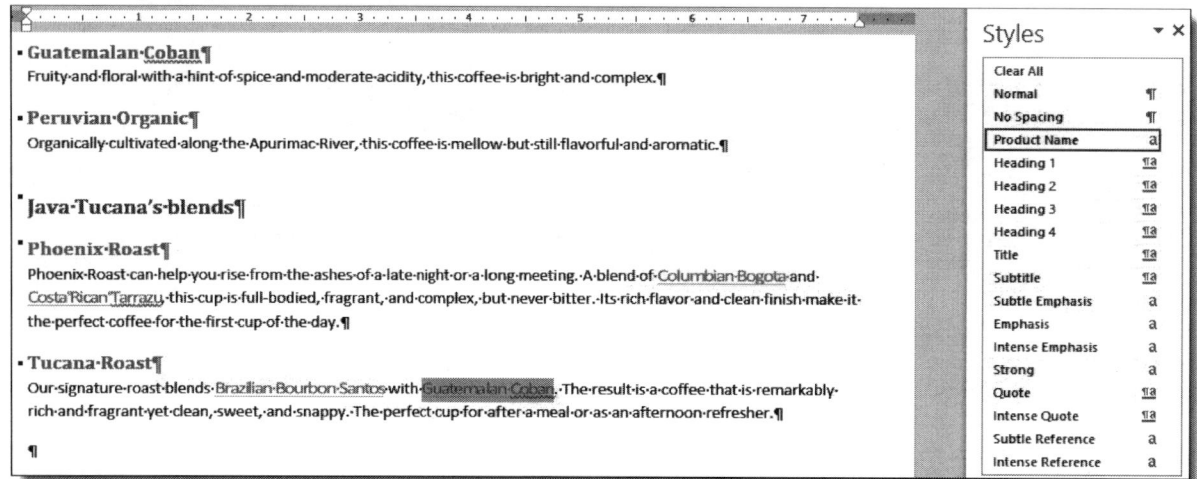

Modifying styles

When you modify an existing style, it automatically updates any text using that style. You can update a style to match selected text, such as some you've manually formatted already. You can also modify it in the Modify Style window, which is almost exactly like the full Create New Style from Formatting window.

Exam Objective: MOS Word Expert 2.2.2

- To update a style that's based on existing text, such as some you've manually modified, right-click the style name, and click **Update <Name> to Match Selection**.
- To freely update a style in the Modify Style window, right-click the style name in either the gallery or the Styles pane, and click **Modify**.

Clearing character formatting

Sometimes it's useful to get rid of all the character formatting on text and start over from the underlying paragraph-level formatting. You can do this quickly by selecting the formatted text, and then pressing **Ctrl+Spacebar**.

Exercise: Modifying a character style

Modify text formatting, update a style to reflect the change.

JT-Coffee-formatting is open and the preceding exercises have been completed.

Exam Objective: MOS Word Expert 2.2.2

Do This	How & Why
1. Observe the coffee names in the Java Tucana blend descriptions.	They are all formatted using the Product Name style.
2. Change the font color for "Columbian Bogota".	
a) Select "Columbian Bogota".	In the Phoenix Roast description paragraph.
b) Change the font color.	Use the Font Color gallery in the Font group on the Home tab. You can change it to any color you like. The text changes color, but the other product names do not. You changed the formatting, but not the style.
3. Change the Product Name style to reflect the new color.	

Word 2016 Level 2

Do This	How & Why
a) Select "Columbian Bogota" again.	
b) In the Styles pane, display the menu for the Product Names style.	Click the arrow to the right of the style.
c) Click **Update Product Name to Match Selection**.	Now, all the product names formatted using the style reflect the change. This is the true power of using style: consistent formatting, and fast changes across an entire document.
4. In the Product Name style's menu, click **Modify**.	To display the Modify Style window. This is another method of modifying a style. Here, you can make changes just as if you were defining a new style.
5. Click **Cancel**.	To close the Modify Style window.
6. Remove the character formatting from "Columbian Bogota".	
a) Select the text.	
b) Press **Ctrl+Spacebar**.	This is a quick way to remove all character formatting from selected text.
7. Return the character formatting to "Columbian Bogota".	You can use the Undo button or reapply the style.
8. Save and close the file.	

Paste options

When you paste content from another location, document, or application, you can use Word's paste options to control exactly how the content is formatted. For example, when you paste content from an Outlook message or just a document with different formatting, you might want to preserve the font of the original document, or you might want to keep only the text, with formatting from the destination document.

Exactly what options are available depends on the type of content you're pasting and what application you've copied it from. In general, you have more options (and potential success) pasting content from other Office applications, but you can paste from a web browser or nearly any other application that lets you select content.

Exam Objective: MOS Word Expert 2.1.6

Paste options from another Word document

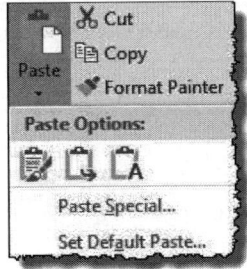

Some paste options you might use include:

Icon	Name	Description
	Use Destination Theme	Pastes the content and styles, but shows the styles using the theme defined for the document. This makes the pasted content match anything already in the document.
	Keep Source Formatting	Pastes the content in Normal style, but with manual formatting from the source document or web page. This preserves the original look as closely as possible, but it's all direct formatting instead of style-based.
	Merge Formatting	Keeps some formatting elements from the source document, while incorporating it with the style in use at the insertion point. For example, this preserves bold text but not necessarily the font or paragraph options.
	Keep Text Only	Pastes only the text itself, without the original formatting. This is often the safest choice when you want to control the formatting in the destination document.
	Paste Special	Opens the Paste Special window, with additional pasting options.
	Set Default Paste	Opens the Word Options window, with settings for the default behavior of the Paste button.

You can point to each option to see a live preview of the results, so you don't need to experiment blindly. Additionally, immediately after you paste content, a clipboard icon appears next to it. Clicking it, or pressing **Ctrl**, opens the Paste Options menu again, in case you've made a mistake.

Paste special

You can choose **Paste Special** from the paste list to view more options.

The Paste Special window, when pasting from an Excel document

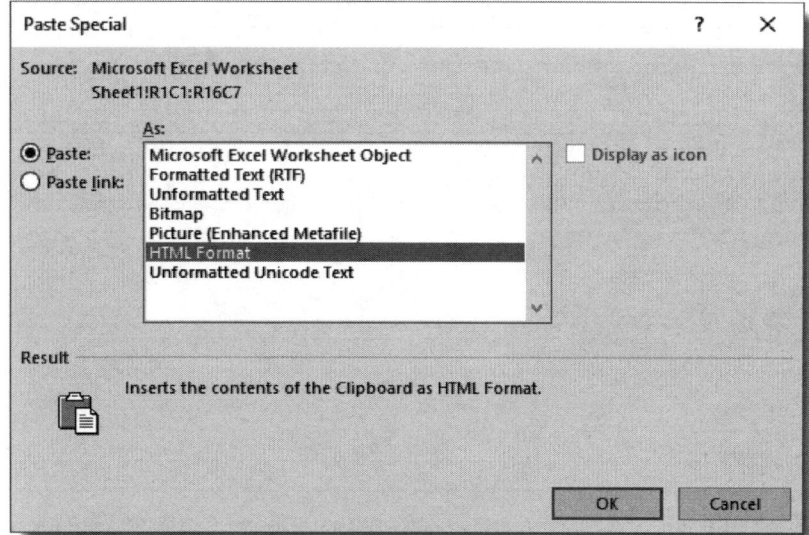

Although the included options vary, depending on what you're pasting, common options include:

- *Microsoft [Office Application] Object*: Place a movable object that's displayed in Word but can be opened and edited in its own application.
- *Formatted text (RTF)*: Preserve formatting using Microsoft's Rich Text Format.
- *HTML format*: Preserve formatting using HTML.
- *Unformatted text*: Paste only the text, without formatting.
- *Unformatted Unicode text*: Like unformatted text, but preserving the larger character set of Unicode fonts.
- *Picture ([Format]):* Paste the content as a graphic, preserving the appearance of the original content. Note that you can't select or edit text once it's been turned into a picture.
- *Bitmap*: Paste the content as an uncompressed graphic. This perfectly preserves the appearance of the copied content, but it can make a very large file size, so it usually isn't ideal.

Additionally, when pasting from another document, you can choose the **Paste Link** option. Although this looks the same as standard pasting, pasting as a link means you can update the source document; the changes are then reflected in the message content.

Exercise: Pasting content

In this exercise, you'll test paste options both from Word documents and external applications.

  Exam Objective: MOS Word Expert 2.1.6

Do This	How & Why
1. Create a new document and save it as `Pasted content`.	You'll practice pasting content into a blank document.
2. Copy some text from another Word document.	
a) Open `About Us`.	
b) Copy all the text on the first page.	From the title down to "local food."
3. Paste the text into the blank document.	
a) In `Pasted content`, click the lower half of the **Paste** button.	
b) Point to [icon].	Don't click it yet. In the Live Preview, the headings and styles are preserved, but instead of the theme colors and fonts in the original document, they use Word's default. **Java Tucana Services** Office coffee service We'll supply your office with early-morn[ing] have whole-bean, ground, and single-se[rve]
c) Point to [icon].	The Live Preview now uses the exact formatting of the source document; however, it would all be pasted as Normal text with direct formatting.
d) Point to [icon].	This option preserves manual formatting such as bold or italic formatting from the original text, but no theme or style information.
e) Point to [icon].	This option pastes only the text itself, with all formatting discarded.
f) Click [icon].	To paste the text with the style information, but using the theme in the destination document (which is the Word default theme in this case).
4. On the Design tab preview different themes and style sets.	Use Live Preview. Because you pasted the content into the destination theme, it changes whenever existing themes or styles change.

Do This	How & Why
5. Insert a page break at the end of the document.	Press **Ctrl+Enter**.
6. Copy content from an Excel workbook.	You'll view paste options when pasting data from another application, in this case, Microsoft Excel.
a) In Excel, open `Sample budget.xlsx`.	
b) Select the entire table, including the logo at the top.	Because of the graphic, it's easiest to click **G16** first and drag up to **A1**. 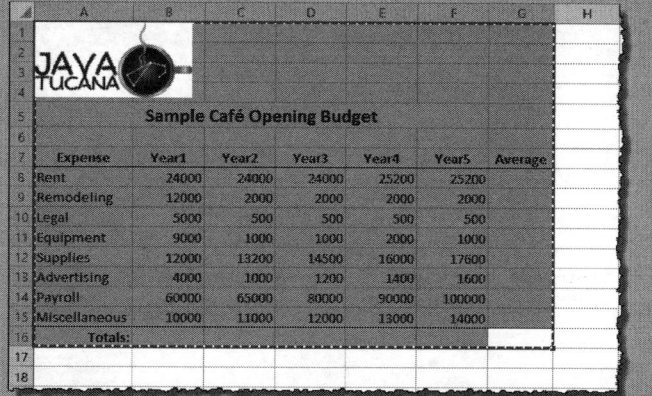
c) Press **Ctrl+C**.	
7. Paste the Excel content into Word.	
a) In **Pasted content**, open the Paste Options list.	The options are different this time. 
b) Point to each option in turn.	In addition to the options you have when pasting from a Word document, you can also paste as a link, either using destination styles or source formatting. You can also paste the content as a picture, but there is no Merge Formatting option.
c) Click **Paste Special**.	The Paste Special window opens. By default, HTML format is selected.
d) Click each option in turn.	There's no Live Preview, but description text appears in the Result section, telling you what to expect.
e) Select **HTML Format** and click **OK**.	The worksheet is pasted as a table, in a fair approximation of how it looked in Excel.
8. Save and close `Pasted content`.	

Do This	How & Why
9. Close all other files without saving.	Close Excel as well.

Assessment: Character styles

Checking knowledge about advanced text formatting.

1. You're creating a document in which all employee names are colored and italicized, and you decide to do so using a style. What style type should you choose?

    - Character
    - Linked
    - Paragraph

2. Which method of creating a style gives you the most control over the formatting included with the style? Choose the one best answer.

    - Creating a style by example
    - Defining a style from scratch

3. When copying text into a document, you want to preserve its layout and font exactly, even if you decide to later change themes in the rest of the destination document. What paste option will take the least amount of work?

    - Keep source formatting
    - Keep text only
    - Merge formatting
    - Use destination styles

Module B: Paragraph styles

You will learn how to:

- Create and modify paragraph styles
- Control the relationships among paragraph styles

Defining paragraph styles

The difference between character styles and paragraph styles is that paragraph styles comprise formatting elements that apply to the paragraph as a whole, such as indents, line spacing, and tabs. Paragraphs can also include font attributes, but again, these will apply to an entire paragraph.

Exam Objective: MOS Word Core 2.2.1

You can create paragraph styles in the same ways you do character styles.

- Format a paragraph as you like, then create the style by example. To do this, place the insertion point within the formatted paragraph, display the menu for the Styles gallery, then click **Create Style**. Name the style and you're done.
- Display the Create New Style from Formatting full window. You can do this by clicking the Modify button in the window displayed by the previous technique, or by clicking the New Style button in the Styles pane. Be sure to specify that you want to create a paragraph style.

Exercise: Creating and using paragraph styles

Format a paragraph, then create a style based on that formatting and use it on other paragraphs.

Exam Objective: MOS Word Core 2.2.1

Do This	How & Why
1. Open `JT-Coffee paragraphs` and save it as `JT-Coffee paragraphs styled`.	This is similar to the document you used to create character styles. You'll format a coffee description paragraph, then create and use a style to format the other descriptions.
2. Set left and right indents for the Brazilian Bourbon Santos description paragraph.	
a) Place the insertion point within the paragraph and display the Paragraph window.	On the Home tab, click the Paragraph Settings button at the bottom of the Paragraph group.
b) Set both the left and right indents to `0.5"`.	The window should look like this.
c) Click **OK**.	To apply the indents. How would you apply these settings to all the other paragraphs? The best way is to use a style.

Do This	How & Why
3. Create a style called **Coffee Descriptions**.	
a) Place the insertion point within the indented paragraph.	
b) Click the Style gallery's dropdown arrow, then click **Create a Style**.	To open the Create New Style from Formatting window.
c) Name the style `Coffee Descriptions`.	This is the simplest, quickest way to create a paragraph style.
d) Click **OK**.	
4. Apply the new style to the other description paragraphs.	
a) Display the Styles pane.	Click the Styles button at the bottom right of the Styles group. You will see the new style in the list.
b) Click within the Columbian Bogota Supremo description, then click Coffee Descriptions.	In the Styles pane. The paragraph is now indented.
c) Apply the style to the rest of the descriptions.	
5. Modify the Coffee Descriptions style so that the indents are .75 inches.	
a) In the Styles pane, right-click **Coffee Descriptions**, then click **Modify**.	The Modify Style window appears, which gives you full control over the definition of the style.

Do This	How & Why
b) Click **Format**, then click **Paragraph**.	
c) Change the left and right indents to `.75"`.	Indentation — Left: 0.75" — Right: 0.75"
d) Click **OK** twice.	Because you modified the style, all of the paragraphs to which the style was applied now reflect the larger indentation.
6. Save the document.	Do not close it.

Relationships among paragraph styles

The relationships among paragraph styles can affect your documents in many ways. Often, you might be unaware of these relationships until you have some unintended consequence that does not, at first, make sense. There are two important types of style relationships to pay attention to.

- Basing a style on another style
- Heading levels

When you create a style, by default it will be based upon the underlying style of the paragraph where the insertion point is, or of the style you are modifying. This gives you a head start, in a sense, on the formatting, because all of the formatting of the base style will already be there for you to build upon. But it also means that if you modify one style, you will be modifying any styles that are based upon it.

This is a good thing in practice. If you create a base style for you document (like the normal style in the default Word template), and then build your styles from there, you will be able to modify the main font for the document simply by changing the font for the base style. But it can lead to sudden changes to dependent styles when you aren't aware of the relationship.

When you use Word's built-in heading styles, you are, in effect, creating a hierarchy of headings in your documents. If you plan to create an outline of your document, or a table of contents, use the numbered heading styles exclusively. That way, you'll have consistent, logical outlines and tables of contents.

Exercise: Exploring relationships among styles

Observe heading levels and the relationship between dependent styles.

`JT-Coffee paragraphs styles` is open.

Do This	How & Why
1. Observe the styles used in the headings.	
a) Click within the title.	The title uses the Title style.
b) Click within the first main heading.	"Single-region South American coffees." This heading and the other main section use the built-in Heading 1 style. This means that these paragraphs will appear at the top level of an outline of the document or of the table of contents.
c) Click within one of the coffee headings.	These headings use the Heading 2 style. Consistent use of heading level styles will result in documents that are well-organized, that look good, and that result in useful outlines and table of contents.
2. Change the color for the "Phoenix Roast" heading.	Select it, then use the Font color gallery to change the color to one you like.
3. Create a new style for the blend headings.	
a) Click within the "Phoenix Roast" heading.	You're going to create a style for the blend headings that is based on the Heading 2 style so you can observe how dependent styles are linked.
b) In the Styles pane, click the New Style button.	To display the Create New Style from Formatting window.
c) Name the style `Blend Headings`.	
d) Observe the Style based on box.	This style is based on the Heading 2 style.
e) Click **OK**.	
f) Apply the style to the other blend heading.	
4. Change the font for the Heading 2 style.	
a) In the Styles pane, right-click **Heading 2** and then click **Modify**.	
b) Select a different font and then click **OK**.	All of the single-region South American coffee headings change, but so do the blend headings. Why is that?
5. Save and then close the document.	

Assessment: Paragraph styles

Checking knowledge about paragraph styles.

1. Paragraph styles cannot be created by example. True or false?

    - True
    - False

2. Which of the following approached to creating styles in a document makes most sense? Choose the one best answer.

    - Create the lowest-level headings first and work backwards to the base style.
    - Create the base style first and build the heading styles from that.

3. All styles are associating with a heading level. True or false?

    - True
    - False

Summary: Styles

In this chapter, you learned how to:

- Use advanced character formatting, create and modify character styles, and use paste options to copy only certain attributes of selected text.
- Create and modify paragraph styles, and understand and control the relationships among those styles.

Synthesis: Styles

In this exercise, you will create character and paragraph styles to use in formatting a menu document.

1. Open `Lunch Menu` and save it as `Lunch Menu styles`.
   This document contains an unformatted menu for a Java Tucana Café.
2. Format one of the item names in a way you like ("Pollo Crazin," for example). Format just the name of the item, and not the price or the paragraph as whole.
3. Create a character style based on the item you just formatted, then apply that style to the other items in the menu.
4. Apply the Title style to "Lunch Menu."
5. Apply the Heading 1 style to "Soups of the Day".
6. Apply the Heading 2 style to the lunch item paragraphs.
7. Does the character style still show on the lunch items after you applied the character style?
8. Create a new paragraph style for the item descriptions, and apply it to the description paragraphs.
9. Modify the description style to be centered on the page.
10. Save and close the document.

The menu formatted using styles

Chapter 4: References and hyperlinks

You will learn how to:

- Create endnotes and footnotes
- Create a table of contents
- Apply a hyperlink

Module A: Reference notes

You can use footnotes and endnotes to cite sources or provide extra information.

You will learn:

- The difference between footnotes and endnotes
- How to insert notes
- How to change note options and note format

Footnotes and endnotes

Exam Objective: MOS Word Core 4.1.1, 4.1.2

Footnotes appear on every page where a note is marked, below a separator line but above the footer area. Endnotes appear at the end of the document, after a separator line.

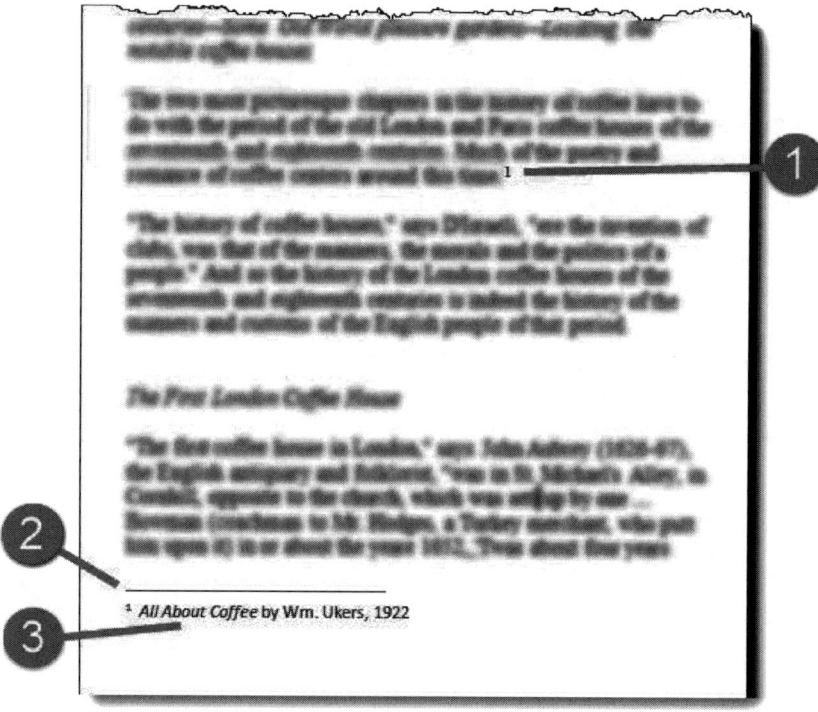

1. Reference mark
2. Separator line
3. Footnote text

After you've added a note, you can view the note text by holding the mouse pointer over the reference mark.

By default, footnotes use Arabic numerals and endnotes use roman numerals, but you can instead use letters, traditional symbols like asterisks and daggers, or define custom symbols using characters from any installed font. Numbering (or lettering) can be continuous or restart for each page or section. You can also change the text style of notes. You can convert footnotes to endnotes or vice versa, or swap all footnotes and endnotes.

Inserting notes

Both footnote and endnote features can be found in the Footnotes group on the References tab. Word automatically keeps track of the numbering or lettering of the notes.

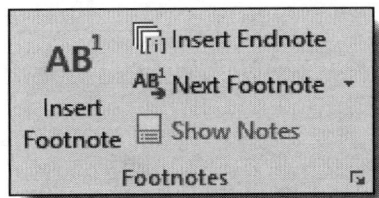

 Exam Objective: MOS Word Core 4.1.1, 4.1.2

1. Place the cursor in the text where you want the note reference.
2. Click **Insert Footnote** or **Insert Endnote**.
   The reference mark is inserted, and a note created at the bottom of the page or the end of the document. The cursor is at the start of the new note.
3. Enter the note text.

If you are adding endnotes to a large document, you can quickly return to your place in the text: just right-click the endnote number, and then click **Go to Endnote**.

Note options

 Exam Objective: MOS Word Core 4.1.1, 4.1.2

You can change the presentation of notes from the Footnote and Endnote window, which you can open in a couple ways:

- Click the dialog box launcher in the Footnotes group on the References tab.
- Right-click a footnote or endnote, and click **Note Options**.

Note: If Word has flagged the note for grammar or spelling (there's a squiggly, colored underline), you won't see note options in the menu when you right-click the note. To ensure you see note-related commands, right-click the reference at the start of the note text.

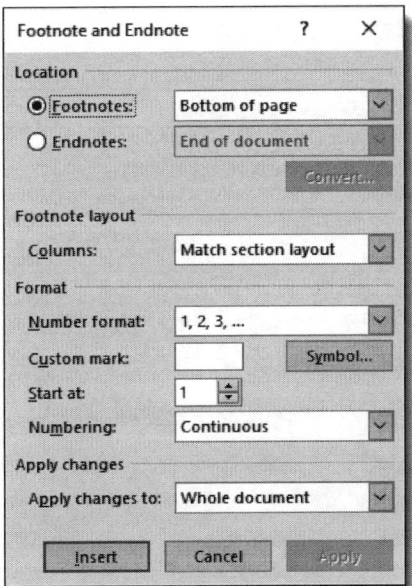

Here are some things you can do from the Footnote and Endnote window:

- Change the location of footnotes and endnotes: footnotes can be at the bottom of the page or right below the text, where the reference mark is. Endnotes can be at the end of the document or the end of each section.
- Convert all endnotes into footnotes, all footnotes into endnotes, or swap all footnotes and endnotes. To convert an individual note, right-click it, and click **Convert to Endnote** or **Convert to Footnote**.
- Select the number format. By default, footnotes use Arabic numbers and endnotes use roman numerals, but you can choose from the following: numbers, upper- and lowercase letters, upper- and lowercase roman numerals, and traditional symbols (asterisk, dagger, double dagger, section symbol).
- Select a symbol to use for the reference mark and corresponding note. If you select a symbol for one note, the next time you add a note, you're prompted to select another symbol or go back to standard marks.
- Set the starting number or letter for notes, and select whether numbering should be continuous or restart at each page or section.

Finally, you set whether any changes should be applied to the whole document or just to the current section.

Changing note format

To configure the formatting of footnote and endnote text and references, modify the styles for these elements.

 Exam Objective: MOS Word Core 4.1.1, 4.1.2

1. Right-click the number at the start of the note text, and then click **Style**.

    The Style window opens with the note text selected.

    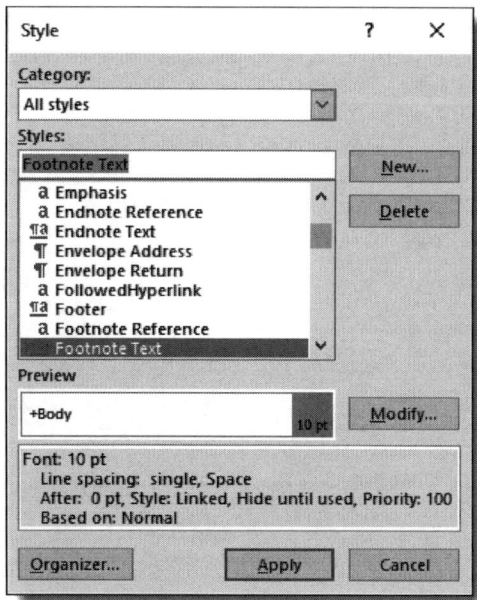

2. Select the style you want to modify.

    If necessary. You can separately modify Footnote Reference, Footnote Text, Endnote Reference, and Endnote Text.

3. Click **Modify**.

    The Modify Style window opens.

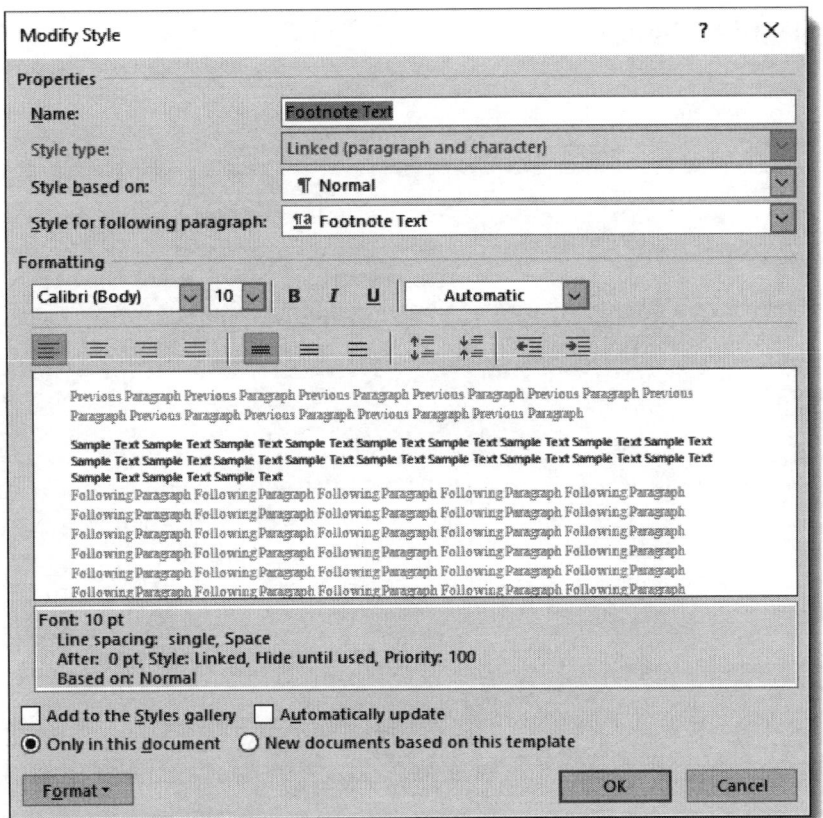

4. Change the formatting options.

   By default, "Only in this document" is selected. You can choose to apply this format to all new documents created from the current template.

5. Click **OK**.

   The formatting is applied to all instances of the style in the document.

6. Click **Apply**.

   To close the Style window.

Exercise: Inserting footnotes and endnotes

 Exam Objective: MOS Word Core 4.1.1, 4.1.2

Do This	How & Why
1. Open `CoffeeHouses` and save it as `CoffeeHouses-notes`.	
2. Place the cursor at the end of the first paragraph.	After the period. You'll add a note marker here.
3. On the References tab, click **Insert Footnote**.	A marker is set, and a new note is made at the bottom of the page. The cursor is there, ready for you to type.
4. Type `Ukers, All About Coffee, p 232.`	*Don't* press Enter.
5. Place the cursor at the end of the second paragraph.	Scroll back up to it.
6. On the References tab, click **Insert Endnote**.	A note is added at the end of the document.
7. Type `Ukers, p 233.`	
8. Right-click the note letter, and click **Go to Endnote**.	You are returned to the note marker in the text.
9. Save and close the file.	

Assessment: Reference notes

1. You insert a footnote or endnote from which tab?
   - Home
   - Insert
   - References
   - Review

2. After entering an endnote, how can you return quickly to your place in the text?
   - Right-click the note text, and click Go to Endnote.
   - Right-click the note number, and click Go to Endnote.
   - Press Ctrl+G.
   - Use the Go To function.

Module B: Table of contents

The automatic table of contents function uses the heading styles in the document to build the table. If the document does not use heading styles, the table of contents can be created manually.

You will learn how to:

- Insert a table of contents
- Use the Table of Contents window
- Change table of contents styles
- Update a table of contents
- Mark image captions
- Insert a table of figures

About tables of contents

Manually assembling a table of contents from a long document can be a lot of work to compile and format, and it easily falls out of date when you edit the body of the document later. Fortunately, Word lets you insert a *table of contents* building block. Each entry in the table is a field reflecting a section of the document and its page.

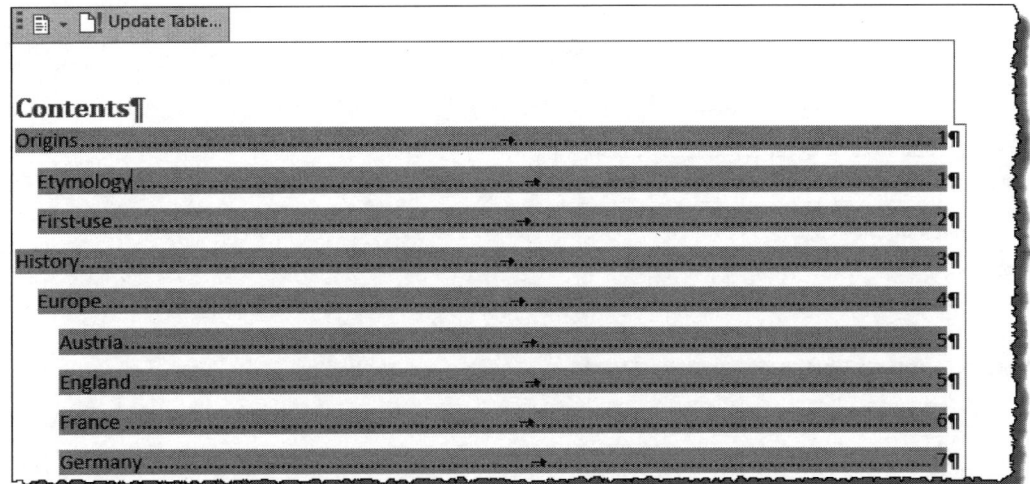

TOC building blocks can be automatic or manual. A manual table of contents is just a formatting framework you enter your own data into. An automatic TOC is more interesting, since each entry is based directly on the content of the document. By default, any text formatted as Heading 1, Heading 2, or Heading 3 appears in the TOC, arranged by level. If you want, you can also include different styles, outline levels, or even table entry fields as TOC entries. Either way, since each entry is generated based on the document, it not only includes an accurate page number, but the entry itself is a hyperlink to the content it references.

Inserting a built-in table of contents

To add a table of contents using default formats, select a built-in table of contents. Typically, you'll want to add it at or near the beginning of the document, but you can place it wherever you like.

 Exam Objective: MOS Word Core 4.2.1

1. Place the cursor where you want to insert the table of contents.
   You might want to add a page break first.

2. On the References tab, click **Table of Contents**.
   To open the Table of Contents gallery.

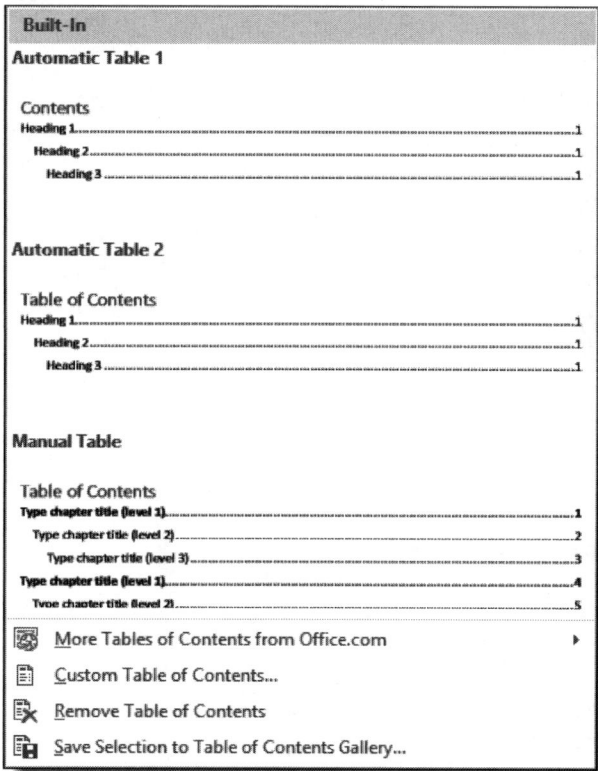

3. Click a style in the gallery.
   - By default, there are two automatic tables, but they differ only in the heading text.
   - If you choose Manual Table, you'll have to fill out the headings and page numbers yourself.

Customizing a table of contents

 Exam Objective: MOS Word Core 3.2.1 and Expert 4.2.1

If one of the table of contents building blocks isn't what you want, you can use the Table of Contents window to access more options. To open it, on the References tab, click **Table of Contents > Custom Table of Contents**.

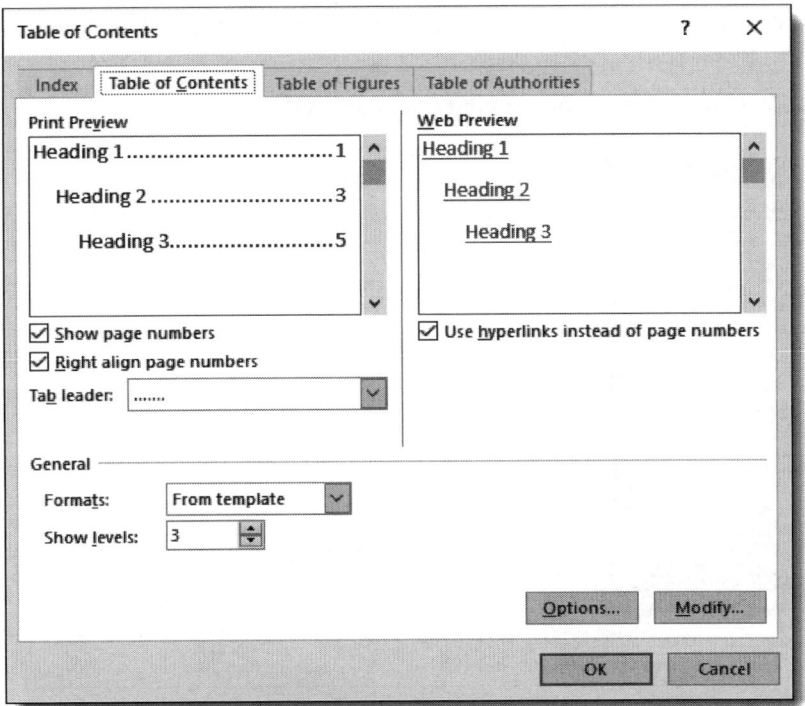

- Change overall table of contents style from the General section.
  - Use the **Formats** list to choose a general appearance.
  - Use the **Show levels** field to choose how many entry levels the table has.
- Change page display options in the Print Preview and Web Preview sections.
  - **Right align page numbers** and **Use hyperlinks instead of page numbers** (for web pages only) are only available if **Show page numbers** is checked.
  - You can only select a tab leader if **Right align page numbers** is checked.
- Click **Modify** to format the text in the table of contents itself. Each Table of Contents entry level has its own associated style, named TOC #.

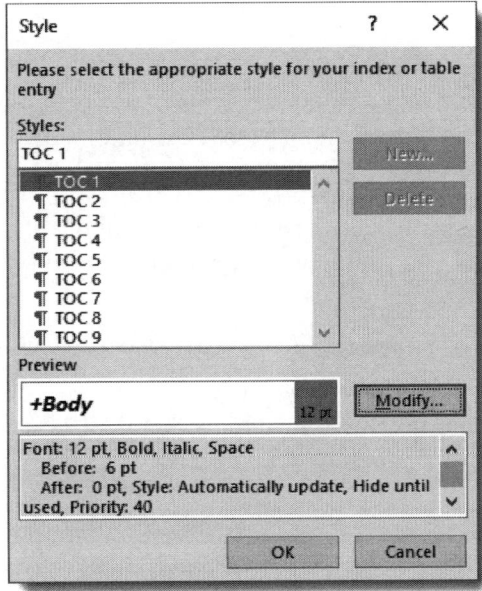

  - To modify a style, click it, then click **Modify**.

- You can only modify TOC styles if you select the **From template** format in the **Table of Contents** window.
- To select exactly what content is used to generate the table of contents, click **Options**.

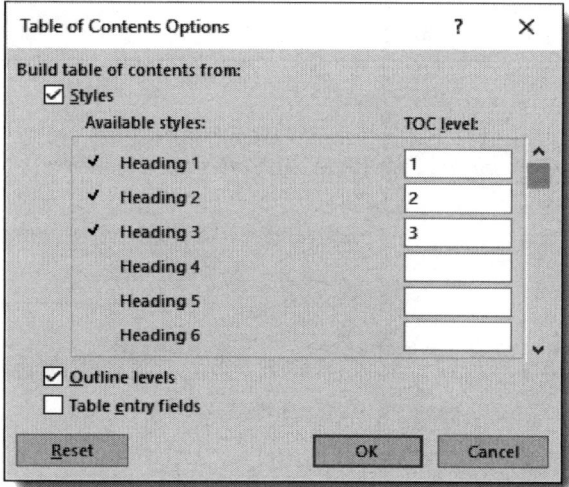

- To base entries on particular styles in the document, check **Styles**.
- To modify which styles are used to generate TOC entries, enter a number in the corresponding **TOC level** field.
- Check **Outline levels** to include styles with assigned outline levels.
- Check **Table entry fields** to include TOC entries that have been manually inserted in the document. Table entry fields are an older and usually obsolete way of creating a table of contents, but they have some uses.
- To save your settings for future use, select the entire table and click **Table of Contents > Save Selection to Table of Contents Gallery**.
- To remove a table of contents, click **Table of Contents > Delete Table of Contents**.

Planning a table of contents

It's easy to insert a table of contents, and it's not even that hard to format one, but if you're not careful you might end up with entries you don't want, or miss entries you do want. You can minimize this problem with document planning, but exactly what you need to do depends on what content your TOC automatically includes.

- If you're basing the TOC off of styles, make sure to apply styles consistently throughout the document. Unless you've assigned TOC styles differently, this means you should use numbered header styles for all text you want to appear in the TOC.
  - You'll need to use as many heading (or other) styles as you have levels in your TOC. You can use other heading styles; they just won't appear in the TOC.
  - By default, heading level and TOC level are the same, but it doesn't have to be that way. You could for example include only Heading 1 and Heading 3 in the TOC, but not Heading 2.

- Click **Add Text** in the Table of Contents group to set a paragraph to a specific TOC level. This will also change its style.

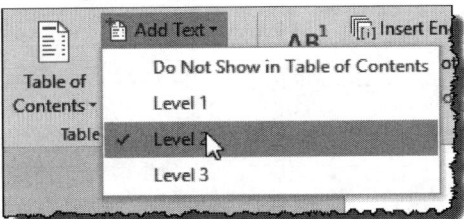

- If you're basing the TOC off of outline levels, make sure to apply outline levels consistently through the document. Remember that you can't change the outline level of a numbered heading style, though you can assign outline levels to other styles.
- If you're using table entry fields, you'll have to manually mark them in the document.
  - To mark a table entry field, place the insertion point and press **Alt+Shift+O** to open the Mark Table of Contents Entry Field window.

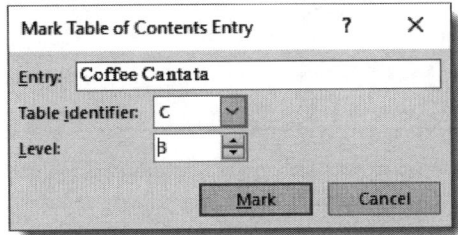

- One good time to use table entry fields is when you want the text in the TOC to be different from the text on the page, such as for an entry name that doesn't directly appear in the document.

Modifying table of contents styles

The Table of Contents window allows you to choose from a few style sets to apply to the table, but you can also format each level individually.

Exam Objective: MOS Word Expert 3.2.1

1. On the References tab, click **Table of Contents > Custom Table of Contents**.
   The Table of Contents window opens.
2. Click **Modify**.
   This opens the Style window, which shows a preview and description of each table of contents level.
3. Select the level you want to change, and click **Modify**.
   The Modify Style window opens.

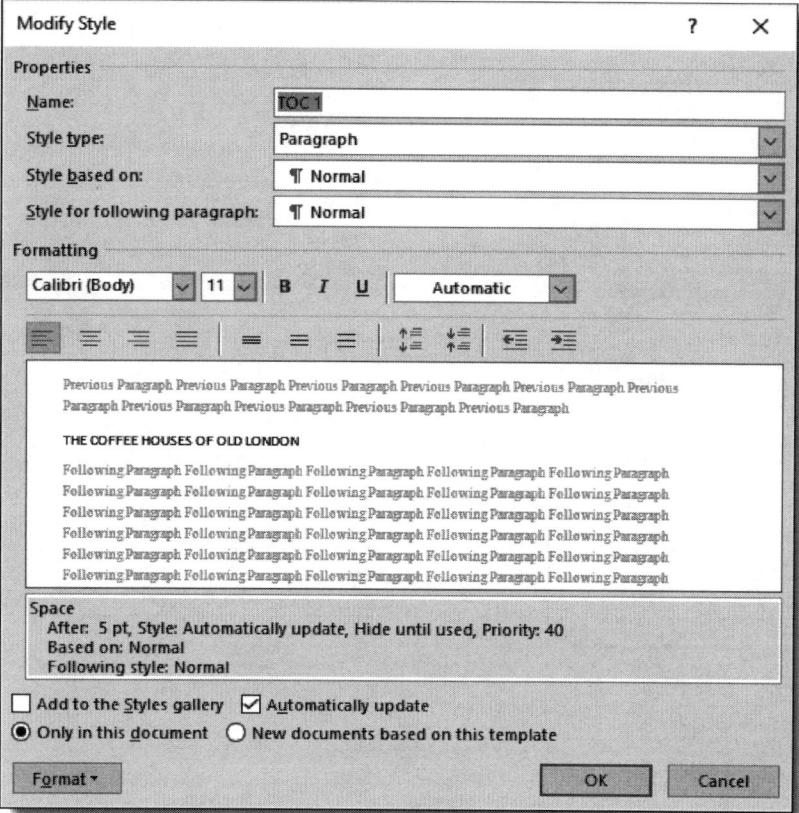

4. Make the changes you want:

   This includes formatting options and whether to apply the style to the current document only or to all new documents created from this template.

5. Click **OK** to return to the Style window, and then click **OK** again.

   You return to the Table of Contents window, where the changes are reflected in the preview.

6. Click **OK**.

   To close the window and apply the style changes.

Updating a table of contents

 Exam Objective: MOS Word Core 4.2.2

If you make changes to your document that alter heading text or move headings to different pages, you can update the table of contents to reflect those changes. If headings have been moved but not changed, you can choose to update the page numbers only. If you've changed the text of the headings, choose to update the entire table.

1. Click anywhere in the table of contents.

   A tab appears at the top of the table.

   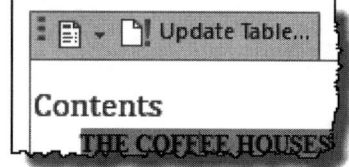

2. Click **Update Table**.

The Update Table of Contents window opens.

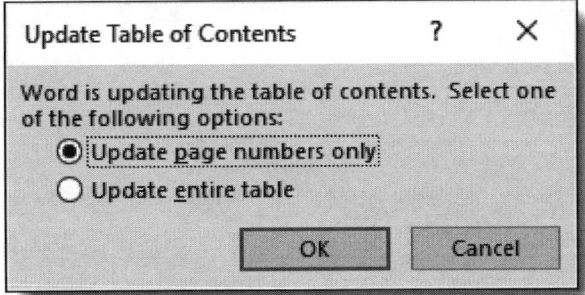

3. Select whether to update page numbers only or the entire table.
4. Click **OK**.

   The table is updated.

Exercise: Adding a table of contents

Exam Objective: MOS Word Core 4.2.1 and Expert 3.2.1

Do This	How & Why
1. Open `History` and save it as `History-toc`.	
2. Insert an automatic table of contents.	
a) Place the cursor on the blank line just below the title.	
b) In the References tab, click **Table of Contents**.	Note the automatic and manual table options. The manual table requires you to fill out the details.
c) Click **Automatic Table 1**.	The table of contents is inserted. It shows three levels of outline detail. The third level shows the Heading 3 styles for the regions under Europe and Asia.
d) Click anywhere in the table.	A tab appears at the top with options.
3. Click **Table of Contents > Remove Table of Contents**.	You'll insert a table with a custom detail level. You could also see this option from the tab on the table.
4. Insert a custom table of contents.	
a) Click **Table of Contents > Custom Table of Contents**.	The Table of Contents window opens.
b) From the Tab leader list, choose _____.	The last option.

Word 2016 Level 2

Do This	How & Why
c) Set "Show levels" to 2.	*[General section showing Formats: From template, Show levels: 2]*
	Heading 3 no longer appears in the preview panes.
d) View the Formats list.	You could choose a variety of presets, but they'd reduce your other customization options.
e) Click **From template**.	To use the default.
5. Set Table of Contents options.	While you don't want Heading 3 to appear in the table, you want to show a couple of other things.
a) Click **Options**.	The Table of Contents Options window opens. By default, the table of contents is built from Heading styles and outline levels.
b) Check **Table entry fields**.	You're going to insert a manual field in the document later.
c) Next to the TOC image caption style, enter 3.	At the bottom of the styles list. *[Dialog showing Title, TOC Heading, ✓ TOC image caption: 3, ☐ Outline levels, ✓ Table entry fields, Reset/OK/Cancel]*
d) Click **OK**.	The Show levels field is no longer visible, and your changes are visible in the Preview panes. *[Preview showing Heading 1....1, Heading 2....3, TOC image caption....5, ✓ Show page numbers, ✓ Right align page numbers, Tab leader:]*
6. Modify the TOC styles.	In contrast to the styles used to build the table of contents, TOC styles control how the table itself is formatted.
a) Click **Modify**.	The Style window opens. The TOC 1 style is selected.

Do This	How & Why
b) Click **Modify**.	The Modify Style window opens, exactly as though you had modified TOC 1 in the Styles list.
c) Click **B**.	To format the style as bold.
d) Click **OK**.	To close the Modify Style window.
e) Open the Modify Style window for TOC 3.	Select it and click **Modify**.
f) Apply italics to the style.	
g) Click **OK** twice.	The changes are reflected in the preview, but the Tab leader was also reset to the default. You'll keep it though.

7. Click **OK**.

To insert the custom table of contents. It doesn't actually show any level 3 entries, but you'll add some.

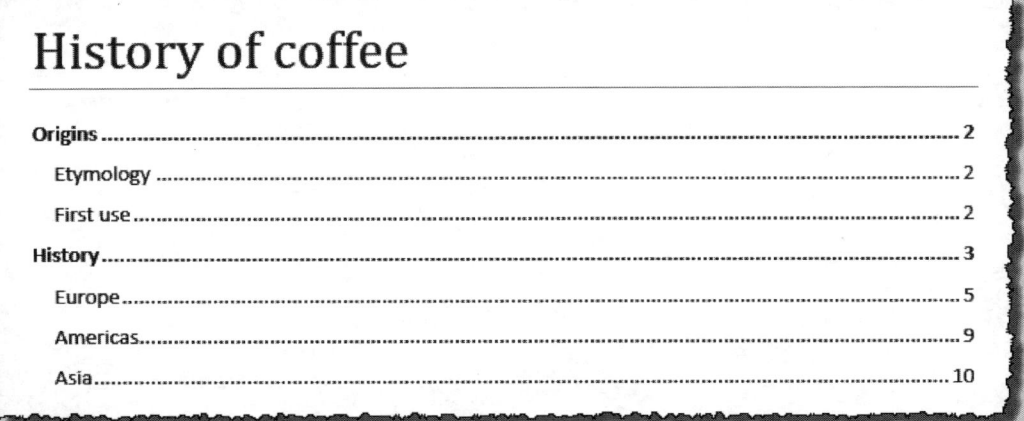

8. Save your new TOC style to the gallery.

a) Select the entire table of contents.	Don't select the document style.
b) Click **Table of Contents > Save Selection to Table of Contents Gallery**.	The Create New Building Block window opens.

Do This	How & Why
c) In the Name field, type `Coffee TOC`.	You'll leave the other settings as is.
d) Click **OK**.	To close the window.
e) Click **Table of Contents > Coffee TOC**.	If you don't do this, Word won't recognize your custom TOC as actually based on the building block. To apply the building block. You're asked whether to update page numbers or the whole table. For now, either will do.
f) Click **OK**.	
9. Add new entries to the table of contents.	
a) At the end of page 3, select the second image caption.	Palestinian women grinding coffee, 1905.
b) Apply the **TOC image caption** style.	Use the Styles gallery. *Palestinian women grinding coffee, 1905* The earliest credible evidence of either coffee d[...]
c) Scroll to the bottom of page 8.	You'll mark the Coffee Cantata in the TOC by adding a table entry field.
d) Click at the beginning of the first line of the quoted text.	Since you're not putting the text itself in the TOC, you can't use a style for this.
e) Press **Alt+Shift+O**.	The Mark Table of Contents Entry window opens.
f) In the Entry field, type `Coffee Cantata`.	
g) In the Level field, type `3`.	The table identifier is C since that's the default for table of contents entries. *Mark Table of Contents Entry dialog: Entry: Coffee Cantata, Table identifier: C, Level: 3*
h) Click **Mark**.	The TC field is inserted. Like any field, you can only see it if formatting is shown.
i) Click **Close**.	To close the Mark Table of Contents Entry window.

Do This	How & Why
10. Update the table of contents.	You entered the changes, but they won't show until you've updated the table.
a) Click anywhere in the table of contents.	Scroll to the top of the document.
b) Click **Update Table**.	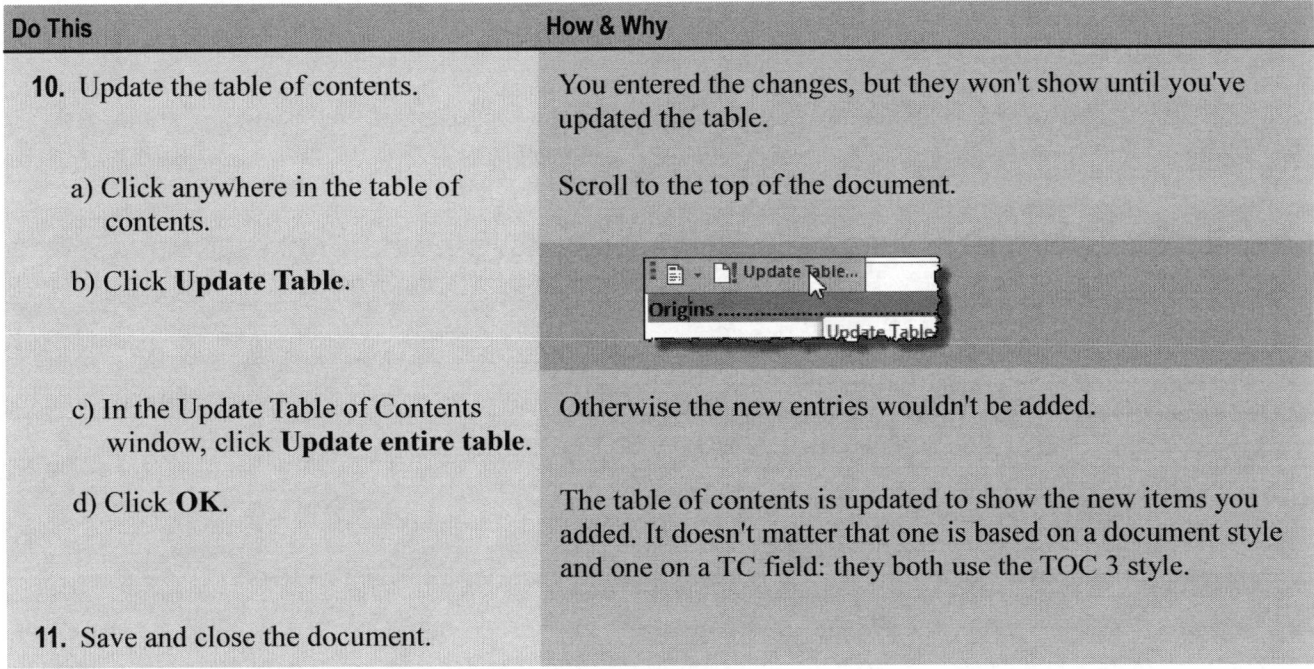
c) In the Update Table of Contents window, click **Update entire table**.	Otherwise the new entries wouldn't be added.
d) Click **OK**.	The table of contents is updated to show the new items you added. It doesn't matter that one is based on a document style and one on a TC field: they both use the TOC 3 style.
11. Save and close the document.	

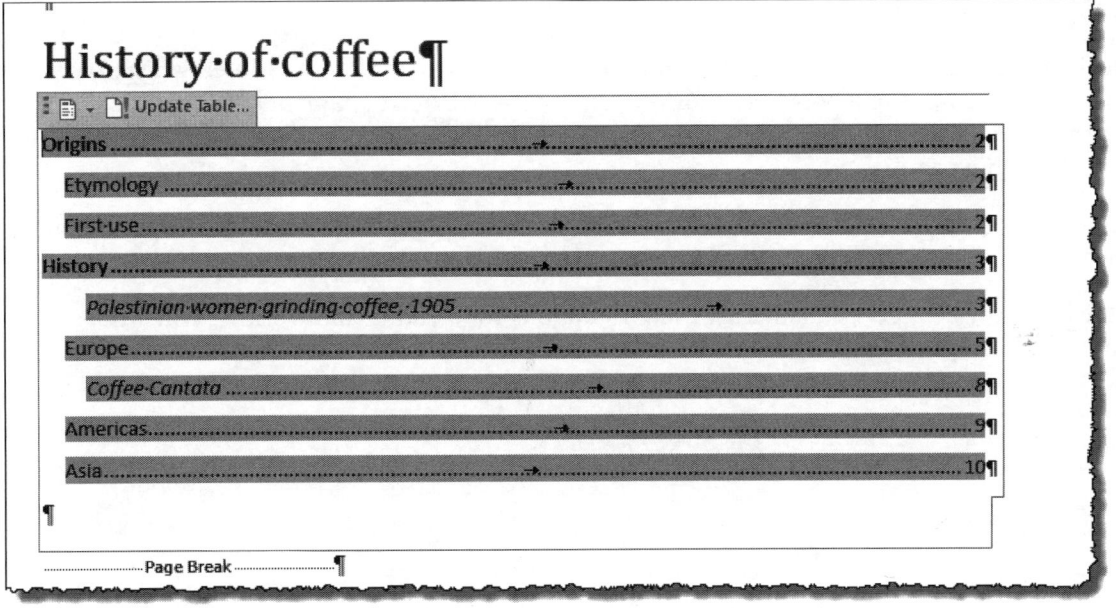

About tables of figures

You can create a table of figures, which lists all the figures in your document, as well as their captions. As with a table of contents, this is particularly useful for large documents with many figures. A table of figures appears and can be formatted very much like a table of contents, but with two major differences.

Exam Objective: MOS Word Expert 3.2.2

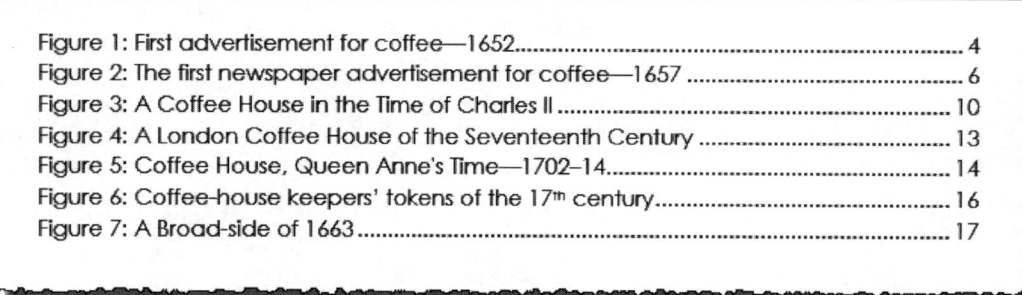

- There is only one level to a table of figures.
- By default, a table of figures isn't based on normal document content. Instead, it's based on captions you insert within the document.

To many people "Table of figures" may conjure mental images of old academic texts printed when graphics were limited and costly additions to a book, but they're pretty useful when a document has important graphical content you want readers to be able to centrally reference. It's not only suitable for pictures, but for formulas, charts, or anything similar.

- To create a table of figures, place the insertion point where you would like the table to appear. On the References tab, in the Captions group, click **Insert Table of Figures**.
- The Table of Figures window contains a variety of options for creating and working with your table. It also contains sections that preview how your table will appear both printed and published on the Web.

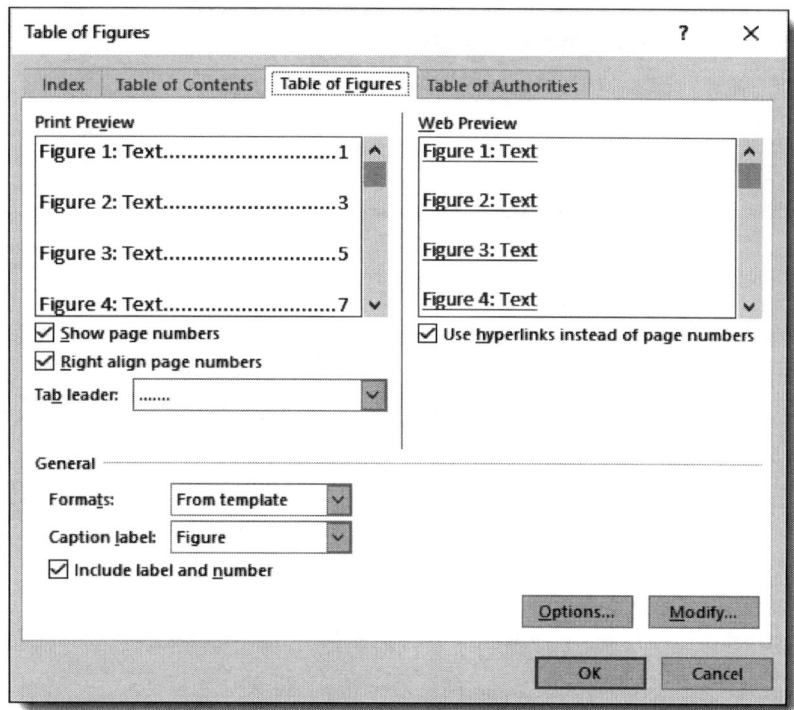

- Click **Options** to set style and field options for the creation of the overall table. Click **Modify** to open the Style window, where you can set the style for the table entries.

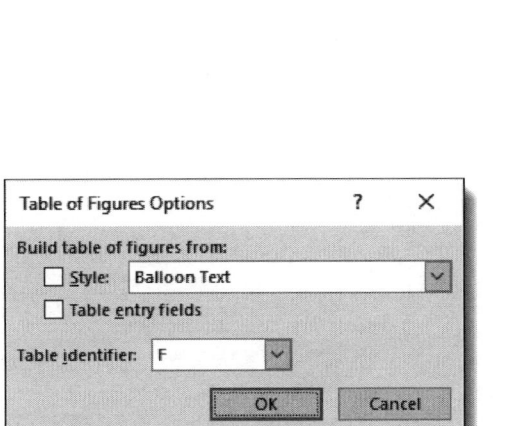
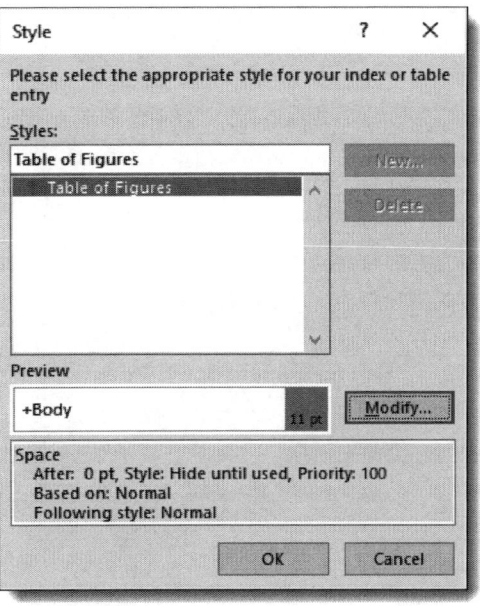

Adding captions to graphics

Adding a caption to a graphic inserts a line of text and an automatic number in the Caption style. Captions are added the same way for most graphical objects, including pictures, shapes, WordArt, SmartArt, and online pictures.

 Exam Objective: MOS Word Core 3.2.1, 4.1.6, 4.1.7

To open the Caption window, either select a graphic, or place the insertion point above or below one. Then click **Insert Caption** on the References tab.

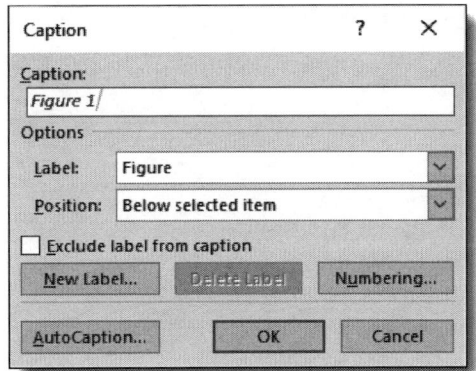

- Type the text of the caption in the Caption field.
- If you began by selecting an item, use the Position list to choose whether to place the caption above or below the graphic.
- By default, each caption has a label and a number.
  - By default, the available labels are **Figure**, **Equation**, and **Table**.
  - Labels aren't just for show: they're also important in generating a table of figures later.
  - To add a new label to the list, click **New Label**.

- Check **Exclude label from caption** to hide the label. The number will still be displayed.
- Click **Numbering** to change caption number formats.
- Click AutoCaption to configure automatic captions for inserted objects.

- Click **OK** when you're finished.

Note that the caption and the shape are not functionally tied, and either can be moved or deleted individually. This can be useful, but also makes it easy to do by accident. If you change the order of captions, the numbers will remain out of order until you update fields. To do this, press **Ctrl+A** to select all text, and then press **F9**.

Inserting a table of figures

Once you've inserted captions for your graphics, you can create the table of figures. To do so, click wherever you want to insert the table, then click **Insert Table of Figures**. You can then configure options in the Table of Figures window.

This table lists captions using the Figure label. It will ignore captions using other labels, but you can also create a table of equations or a table of tables from the same window. Overall, it's very similar to inserting a table of contents.

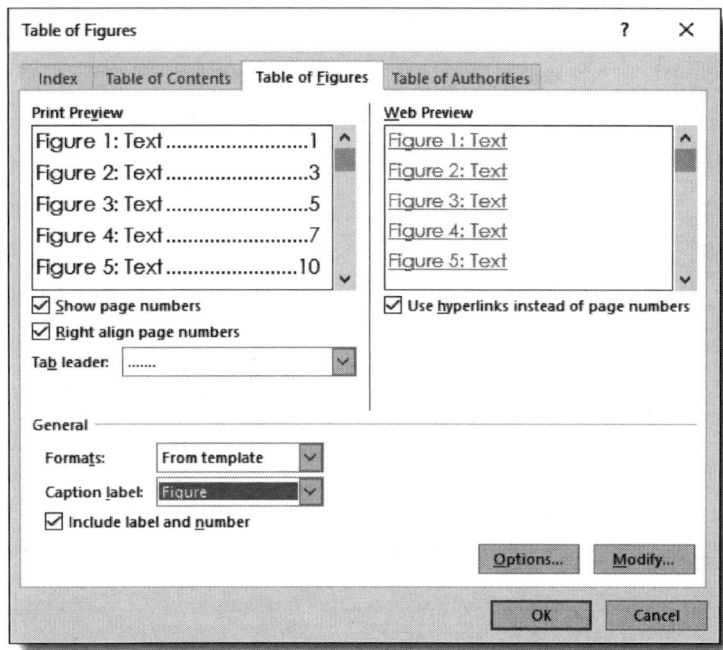

One important thing about a table of figures is that it only includes captions with one type of label. For example, a table of figures can have Figures or Equations, but not both. If you use multiple labels in a single document, each needs its own table.

- Choose the label type from the **Caption label** list.
- Change overall appearance from the General section.
    - Use the **Formats** list to choose a general appearance.
    - Clear **Include label and number** to show only the caption for each item.
- Change page display options in the Print Preview and Web Preview sections.
    - **Right align page numbers** and **Use hyperlinks instead of page numbers** (for web pages only) are only available if **Show page numbers** is checked.
    - You can only select a tab leader if **Right align page numbers** is checked.
- Click **Modify** to format the text in the table of figures itself. Unlike a table of contents, there is only one default Table of Figures style.
- Click **Options** to generate the table of figures from styles or table entry fields.

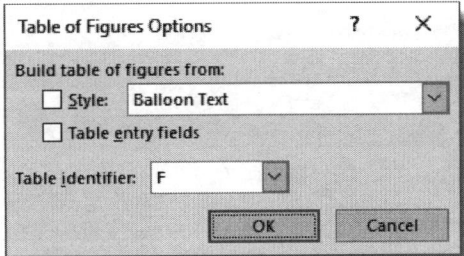

- Click **OK** when you're finished to insert the table.

You can also update a table of figures in much the same way that you can a table of contents. Click anywhere in the table, then click **Update Table** in the Captions group.

Exercise: Adding a table of figures

In this exercise you'll define captions in a document, then create a table of figures.

Do This	How & Why
1. Open `History` and save it as `History-figures`.	
2. Add a caption.	
a) Click the advertisement image at the top of page 6.	To select it. It already has a caption, but that's just ordinary text so wouldn't show up in a table.
b) On the References tab, click **Insert Caption**.	The **Caption** window opens.
c) From the Label list, select **Figure**.	If necessary.
d) From the Position list, select **Below selected item**.	If necessary.

Chapter 4: References and hyperlinks / Module B: Table of contents

Do This	How & Why
e) Edit the Caption field to read `Figure 1: First advertisement for coffee - 1652`.	"Figure 1" is inserted automatically.
f) Observe the window.	You could change or hide the label, or change the numbering scheme, but you'll keep the defaults.
g) Click **OK**.	The caption is inserted.
3. Delete the paragraph below the new caption.	The "1652 advertisement for St. Michael's Alley" text.
4. Insert more captions.	You'll add a couple more captions before inserting a table of figures.
a) Insert a caption for the image at the top of page 5.	Select the image, then click **Insert Caption**.
b) Name the caption `Dutch engraving of Mocha - 1692` and click **OK**.	
c) Delete the pre-existing caption.	Below the one you just inserted.
d) Add a caption to the image at the bottom of page 3.	Palestinian women grinding coffee. Don't forget to delete the existing caption.
5. Insert a table of figures.	
a) Place the cursor on the blank line just below the title.	

Do This	How & Why
b) In the Captions group, click **Insert Table of Figures**.	The Table of Figures window opens.
c) From the Formats list, choose **Formal**.	The new format is reflected in the preview panes.
d) Clear **Show page numbers**.	The tab leader disappears, and Right-align page numbers is disabled.
e) Check **Show page numbers**.	You'd rather display them.
f) Click **OK**.	

To insert the table.

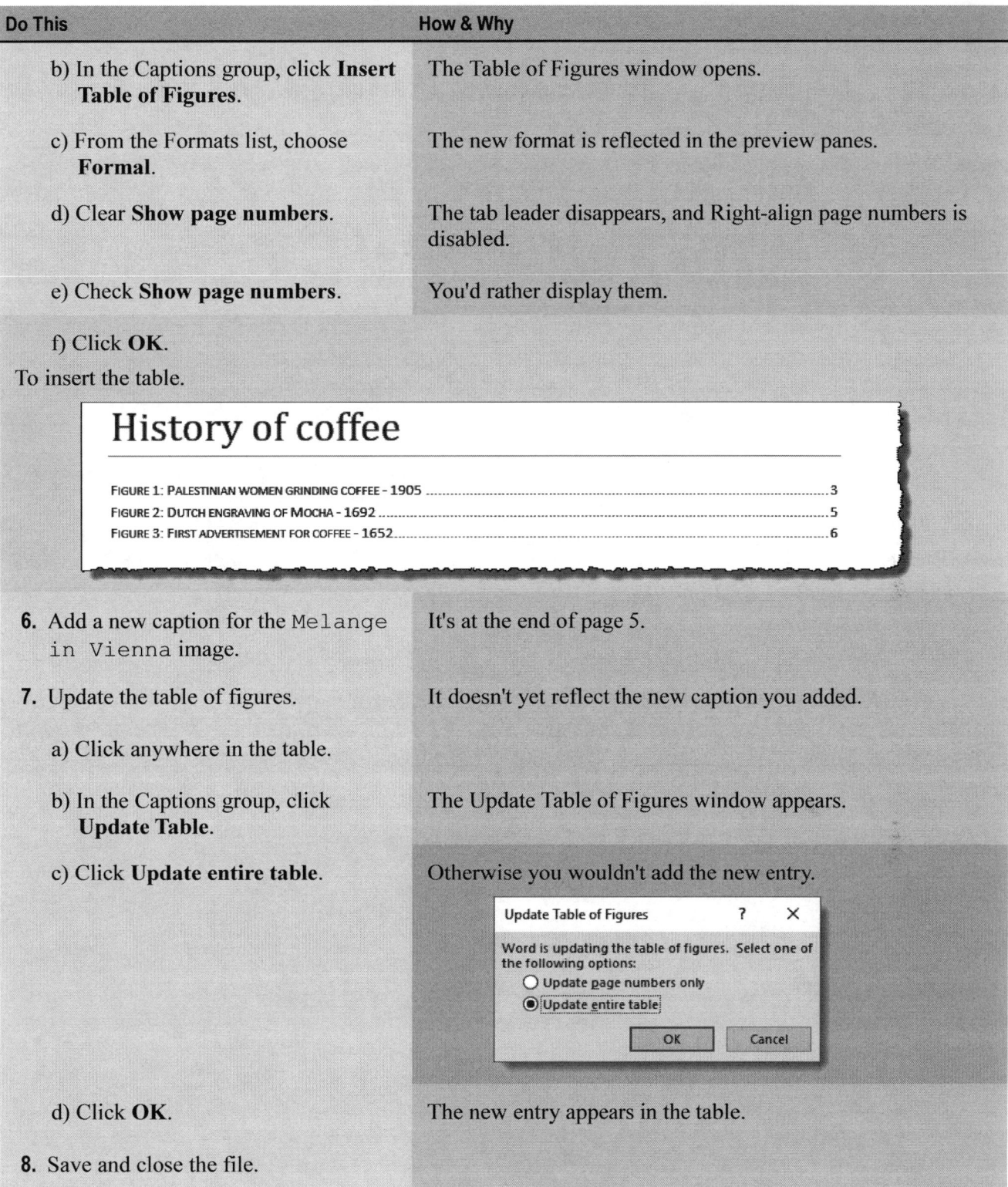

6. Add a new caption for the `Melange in Vienna` image.	It's at the end of page 5.
7. Update the table of figures.	It doesn't yet reflect the new caption you added.
a) Click anywhere in the table.	
b) In the Captions group, click **Update Table**.	The Update Table of Figures window appears.
c) Click **Update entire table**.	Otherwise you wouldn't add the new entry.
d) Click **OK**.	The new entry appears in the table.
8. Save and close the file.	

Assessment: Table of contents

1. If you don't use heading styles in a document. you can fill out the table of contents manually. True or false?

    - True
    - False

2. Which option in the Table of Contents window determines what heading levels are shown?

    - Heading level
    - Formats
    - Heading depth
    - Show levels

Module C: Hyperlinks

You can apply a hyperlink to just about any object in a Word document that you can select, including text, pictures, shapes, and SmartArt.

You will learn:

- How to apply different types of hyperlinks

Applying hyperlinks

 Exam Objective: MOS Word Core 1.2.2

To apply a hyperlink, right-click an object, and click **Hyperlink**. If the object already has a hyperlink, you'll see options to edit, select, open, copy, and remove the hyperlink.

If you want to apply a hyperlink to a phrase or sentence, you need to select the words first. Then, either right-click the selection and click **Hyperlink**, or on the Insert tab's Links group, click **Hyperlink**. In the Insert Hyperlink window, the display text is the same as the selected text by default, but you can change that. For instance, you could change the display text of an email address read "Email Me" instead of the actual address.

Note: If you right-click a word or phrase that has been flagged as a misspelling or grammatical error, you'll see a correction-related menu, and it won't have the hyperlink option.

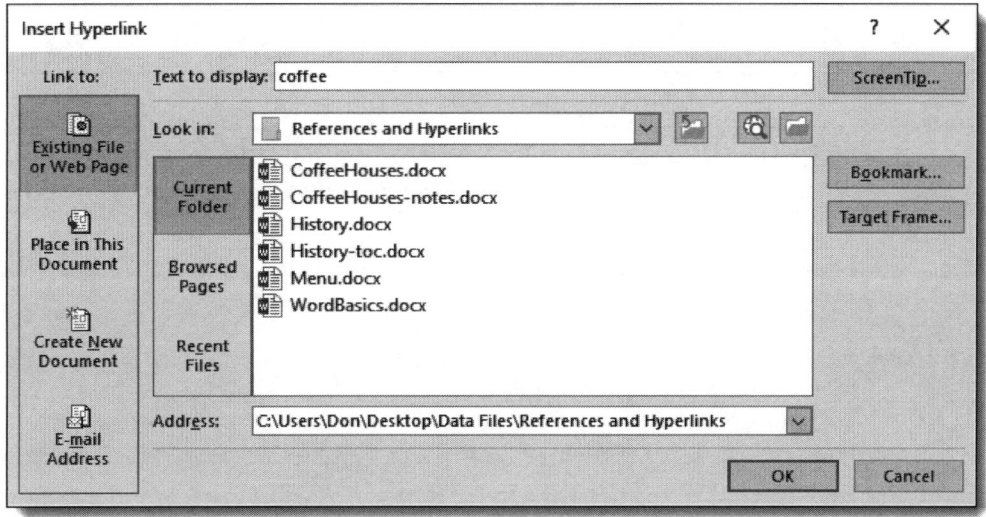

Here are the general categories of hyperlink that you can add to your document.

Hyperlinks

Type of link	Description
Existing File or Web Page	Enter the URL of a web page or the path to a file on your computer or network. You can browse for the file, and there are options to see files in the current folder, recently browsed pages, and recently opened documents. Click **Bookmark** to use a hyperlink as a bookmark for a section in the document.
Place in This Document	Choose from a list of headings in the document. Following the link jumps to that place in the document. This is the same as creating a bookmark hyperlink.
Create New Document	When the link is followed, it opens a new document in Word. You can create the document at the time you create the link, or it can be created when a user follows the link. If you don't specify a file name and location, it uses a default file name and the same location as the current document.
E-mail Address	Enter an email address and (optionally) a subject line. When the link is followed, a new message is started using the address and subject in the link. This requires the computer to have an installed email client such as Microsoft Outlook.

You can follow links in a Word document by holding down **Ctrl** and clicking the link. If you save the document as a web page, though, the link works with just a single click. Remember that links to local resources do not work on another computer unless those resources go along with the document and are in the same relative location.

Exercise: Applying a hyperlink

Exam Objective: MOS Word Core 1.2.2

Do This	How & Why
1. Open `Menu` and save it as `MenuLinks`.	
2. At the bottom of the menu, select www.javatucana.com.	D CUP OF SOUP COMBO $7 es, visit us at www.javatucana.com or email
3. Right-click the selection, and then click **Hyperlink**.	
4. Enter the information for the hyperlink:	The URL in the document is a hyperlink.

Do This	How & Why
a) Under Link to, ensure that either Existing File or Web Page is selected. b) In the Address field, enter `http://www.javatucana.com`. c) In Text to display, enter `www.javatucana.com`. d) Click **OK**.	Do this second because changing the address field will change this field.
5. Create a hyperlink for the email address:	For daily specials, catering, a info@javatucana.com. The link is created. If it's not what you wanted, right-click it, and click **Edit Hyperlink**. You can hold down **Ctrl** and click the links if you want to test them, but you'll need an Internet connection and an installed mail client for both to work correctly.
a) Select the email address, right-click it, and click **Hyperlink**. b) Under Link to, click **E-mail Address**. c) Fill out the text to display, the email address, and the subject line. These can be whatever you like. d) Click **OK**.	
6. Save and close the document.	

Assessment: Hyperlinks

1. Hyperlinks can be applied only to text. True or false?

    - True
    - False

2. Which method(s) allow(s) you to create a hyperlink to another location in the same document?

    - Use the Place in This Document link.
    - Use Existing File or Web Page, then click Target Frame.
    - Use Existing File or Web Page, then click Bookmark.
    - Use Create New Document, then click Bookmark.
    - Use Create New Document, then click Target Frame.

3. For email addresses, the display text is always the same as the address. True or false?

    - True
    - False

Summary: References and hyperlinks

You should now know:

- The difference between footnotes and endnotes, how to insert footnotes and endnotes, and how to change note options and formatting
- How to insert a table of contents, use the Table of Contents window, change table of contents styles, and update a table of contents
- How to apply different types of hyperlinks

Synthesis: References and hyperlinks

1. Open WordBasics and save it as WordBasics-ref.
2. Place the cursor at the beginning of the document, before the title.

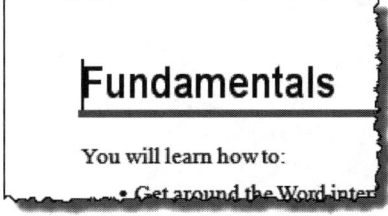

3. On the References tab, click **Table of Contents > Custom Table of Contents**.
4. Insert a table of contents with these settings:
   - Show levels: 4
   - Formats: Classic
   - Leader: Dots
5. For each of the three objectives under the title, apply a hyperlink to the corresponding module.
   In the Insert Hyperlink window, select **Place in This Document**, and then select the module from the list of headings. The first objective links to Module A, the second to B, and the third to C.
6. Add a footnote after the title. The footnote should read From Word 2010 Level 1, copyright 2015.
7. Save and close the document.

Chapter 5: Navigation and organization

You will learn how to:

- Navigate large documents
- Use master documents

Module A: Navigating documents

You will learn how to:

- Use the Navigation pane
- Use advanced find and replace features
- Use the Go To and Browse by features

The Navigation pane

To open the Navigation pane, press **Ctrl+F**, or click **Find** on the Home tab, or check **Navigation Pane** on the View tab. The pane opens on the left side by default, but you can drag it to another location, including outside the Word window. There are three tabs in the Navigation pane: Headings, Pages, and Results.

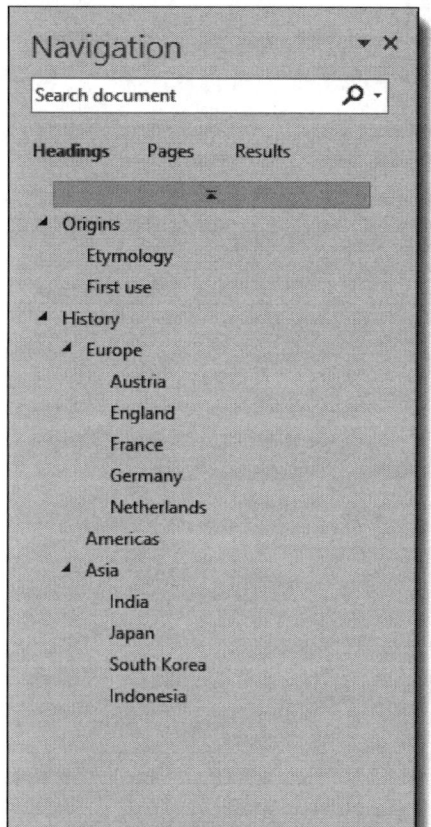 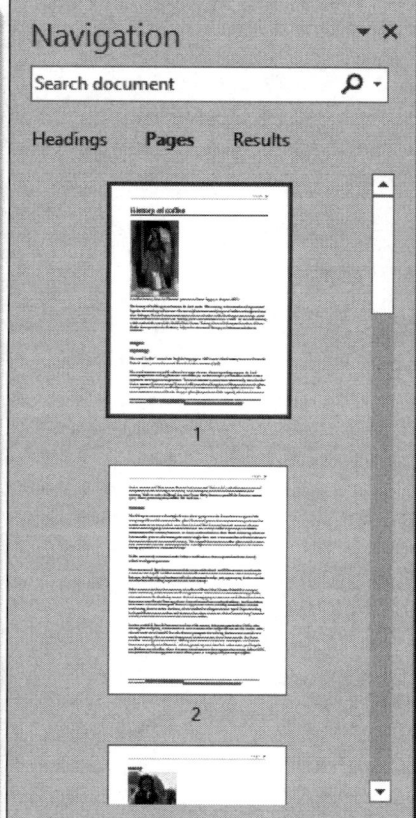 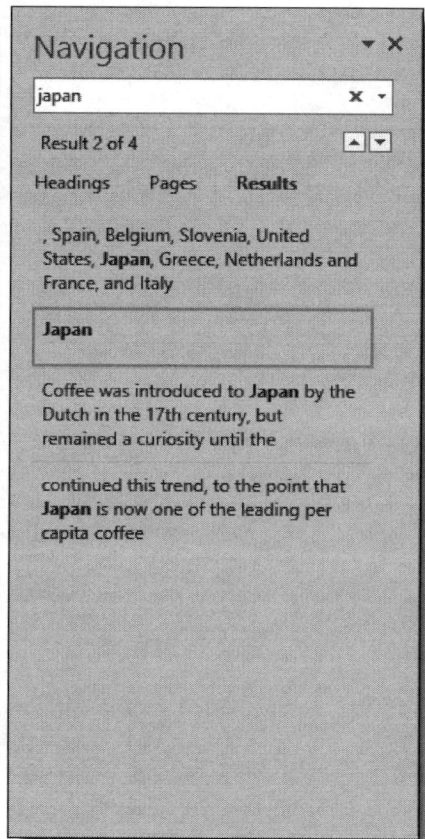

The Headings tab shows an outline of the document based on the headings styles used in it. Headings can be dragged to a new location to reorganize the document. The Pages tab shows a miniature of each page, and the Results tab shows you the context of each instance of what is entered into the search box at the top of the pane. Note that if there are too many instances of a search term in the document, the Results tab does not show them, though they are highlighted in the document.

The Find and Replace window

Exam Objective: MOS Word Core 2.1.1

The Navigation pane is adequate for many text searches, but the Find and Replace window offers a lot more control and options. To open it from the Home tab, click **Replace**, or click the arrow to the right of the Find button, and select **Advanced Find**. Both open the Find and Replace window, but to different tabs.

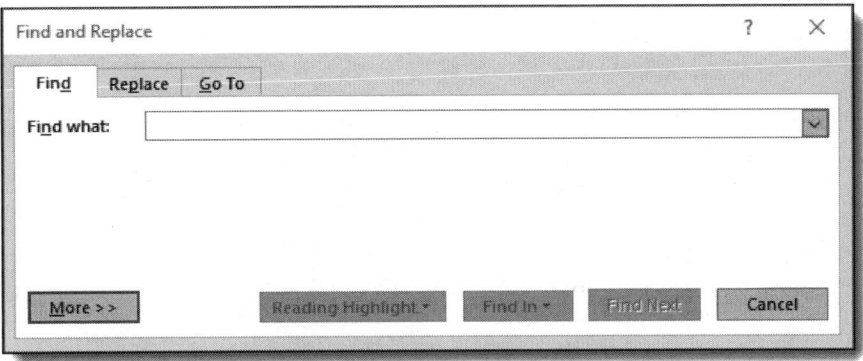

Using advanced find features

Exam Objective: MOS Word Core 2.1.1, 2.1.2 and Expert 2.1.1

When you first open the Find and Replace window, the search options are hidden. You have to click the **More>>** button to access the power of the advanced find features.

1. On the Home tab, click the arrow on the right of the Find button, and click **Advanced Find**.
   The Find and Replace window opens.
2. Click **More>>** to see more options.

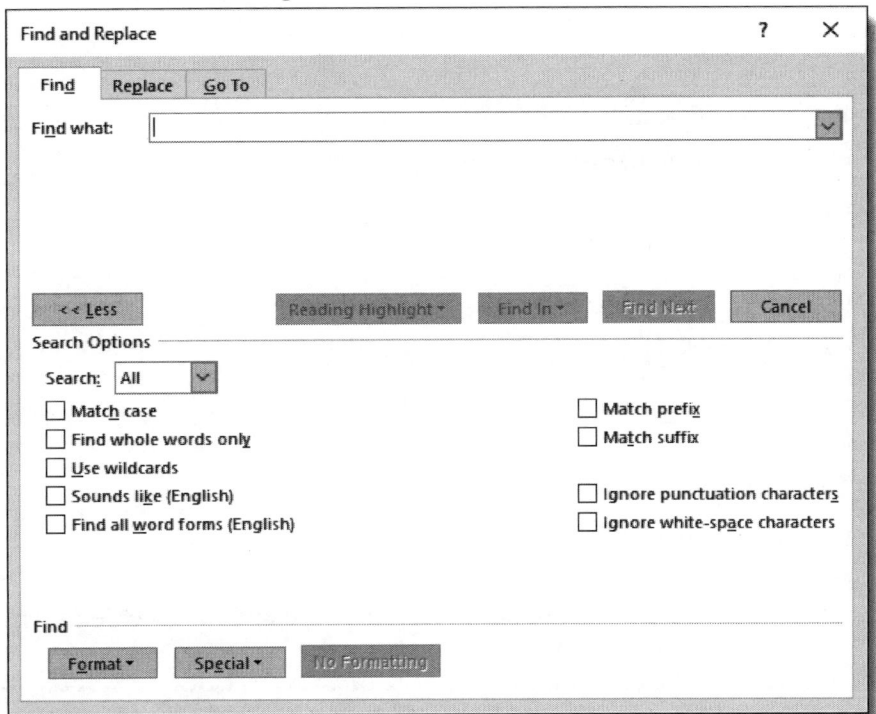

Word 2016 Level 2

3. Enter the term you want to search for.
   Case doesn't matter unless you set that as an option.

4. If you want to highlight the terms, click **Reading Highlight**.
   You can also clear previous highlighting.

5. If you want to want to limit what text is searched, click **Find In**.
   You can limit the search to selected text, the main document, or the headers and footers.

6. Check any search options you want applied.
   Under Search Options, you can, for example, select **Match case** to search for text that appears exactly as typed.

7. To find text with specific formatting, click **Format**, and select the formatting you want.
   You can search for a formatting type without even specifying text to find. So, for instance, you can search for instances of a certain header style, regardless of the text. Or, select **Use wildcards** to find text that appears exactly as typed but that also include occurrences indicated by wildcard characters. Common *wildcards* are ? (any single character or space; for example, typing "t?p" finds "tap," "tip," "top," "t p") and * (any string of characters; for example, "b*t" finds "bat," "bit," "burst," "broadsheet").

8. To search for special characters that are not easy to enter, such as paragraph characters or footnote marks, click **Special**, and select the character.

9. To clear previously specified formatting, click **No Formatting**.

Replacing text

The Replace tab has all the same options as the Find tab, with the exception of the highlight feature.

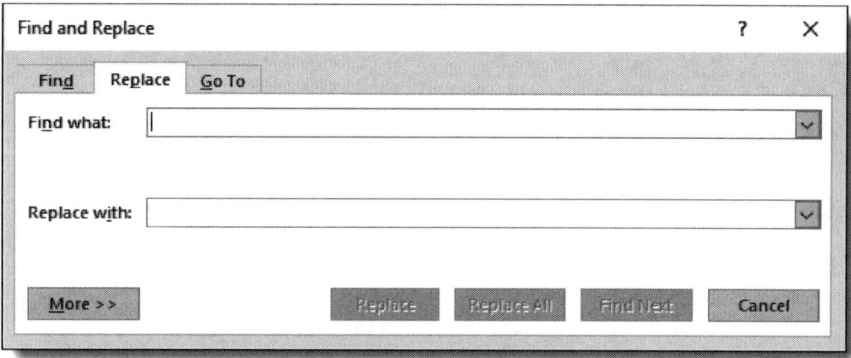

 Exam Objective: MOS Word Core 2.1.1, 2.1.2 and Expert 2.1.1

1. On the Home tab, click **Replace**.
   The Find and Replace window opens to the Replace tab.

2. Enter the text you want to find and the text you want to replace it with.

3. Click **More>>** if you want to set more options.

4. Set the search options.
   These apply to the text being searched for.

5. If you want, select formatting or special characters.
   These apply to the replacement text only.
   Note: If you want to use Formatting or Special buttons in both the Find and Replace fields, you can switch between the Find and Replace tabs. The values in the fields are preserved.

Using Go To

Unlike the find feature, the Go To tab in the Find and Replace window does not search for text but for types of objects.

 Exam Objective: MOS Word Core 1.2.4

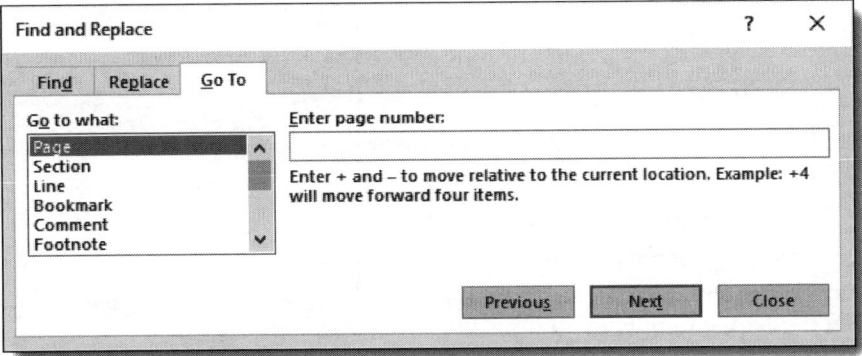

1. On the Home tab, click **Replace**.
    To open the Find and Replace window.
2. Click the **Go To** tab.
3. From the list, select the object type to search for.
4. Enter the number of the object to go to.
    This refers to the order of the objects in the document. The third graphic is number 3, but it does not need to be explicitly labeled. You can also enter + or − and a number to move relative to the current object.
5. Click **Go To**.
    This appears only if you enter a number. You don't need to enter a number to go to the next or previous object.

Finding specific document elements

You can use the Navigation pane to search for different types of document elements, such as graphics, equations, tables, footnotes/endnotes, and comments.

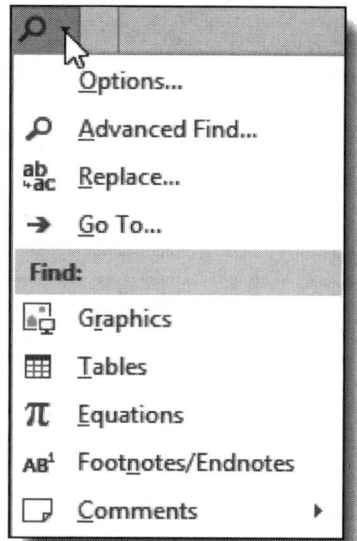

1. Open the Navigation pane.
   On the View tab, in the Show group, click **Navigation Pane**.

2. At the right of the Search box, click the down arrow.
   A menu appears, displaying search options and categories.

3. Under Find, click the icon of the object you want to search for.
   For example, clicking Graphics finds any graphics in a document, stopping at and selecting the one that it finds first from the initial position of the insertion point. In the Navigation pane, the results are numbered, and up and down arrows allow you to navigate through the results found.

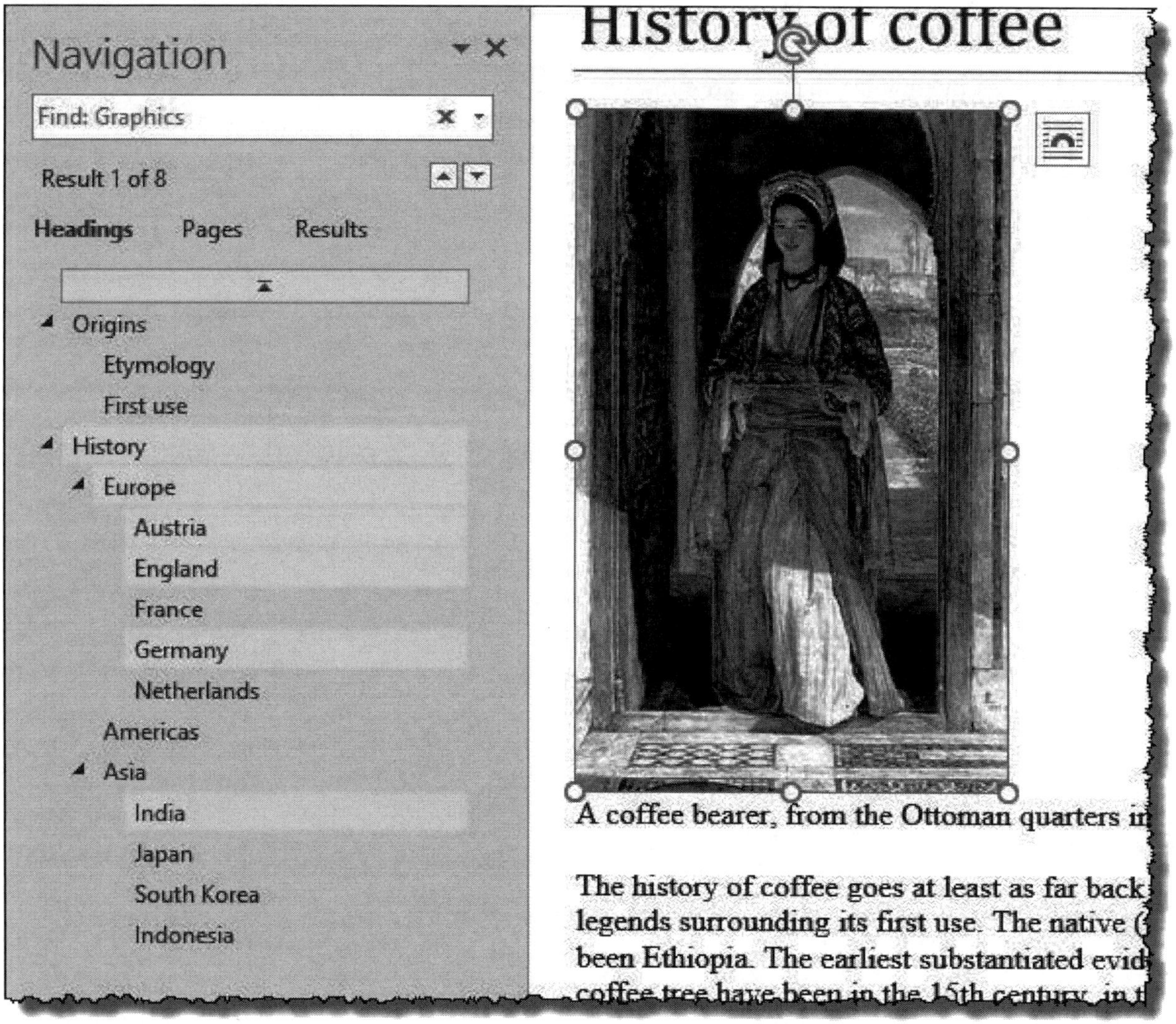

Exercise: Navigating a document

Do This	How & Why
1. Open `CoffeeHistory` and save it as `CoffeeHistory-nav`.	
2. On the Home tab, click **Find**.	To open the Navigation pane. Clear any previous search terms, if there are any.
3. In the Navigation pane, click the **Headings** tab.	It's the first one. You can see the headings in the document.
4. Click the **Pages** tab.	Scroll down to see miniatures of the pages.
5. One the Home tab, click the arrow next to Find, and click **Advanced Find**.	To open the Find and Replace window.
6. Click the **Replace** tab and then the **More>>** button.	Observe the options.
7. Click **Format**, and then **Special**.	To see the options available.
8. Replace all instances of "coffee" with "tea."	
a) In the "Find what" box, enter `coffee`.	
b) In the "Replace with" box, enter `tea`.	
c) Click **Replace All**.	A message tells you how many instances have been replaced.
d) Click **OK**, and close the Find and Replace window.	
9. Observe the document.	It is now a very inaccurate history of tea. Note that when you don't specify case, Word replaces capitalized words with the same case, as in the document title.
10. Close the document without saving.	Why would you want to save this?

Assessment: Navigating documents

1. In the Find and Replace window, which do you click to search for special characters such as footnote marks and paragraph characters?

    - Special
    - Format
    - Symbol
    - Character

2. Which features allow you to skip through instances of a specified object, such as pictures or headings?

    - Skip To
    - Go To
    - Find Object
    - Hop Along
    - Navigation pane Search box

3. Which keyboard shortcut opens the Navigation pane?

    - Alt+N
    - Ctrl+F
    - Ctrl+N
    - Alt+F

Module B: Master documents

You will learn how to:

- Insert a subdocument into a master document
- Organize your subdocuments in a logical manner

Master documents and subdocuments

If you are working on a large, multi-part document, or have multiple authors working on a project, you might want to use a master document with subdocuments. The master document is a Word file that contains references or links to subdocuments, each of which is another Word file.

There are a few important points to keep in mind when working with master documents and subdocuments.

- While you are working in the master document, it is not obvious that different parts are coming from different files, unless you are in Outline view. Otherwise, a master document behaves like any other document.
- Page numbering is continuous, and you can create a table of contents or index based on the whole document.
- Changes you make to content in the master document are saved in the subdocument that content comes from.
- You can expand and collapse the subdocuments in Outline view, and rearrange the order of the subdocuments.

Inserting subdocuments

There's nothing special about a master document; it's just a regular Word document. What makes it a master document is that is has subdocuments. You insert the subdocuments in Outline view.

1. On the View tab, click **Outline**.

    The Outlining tab opens.

2. Click **Show Document**.

    To expand options in the Master Document group.

    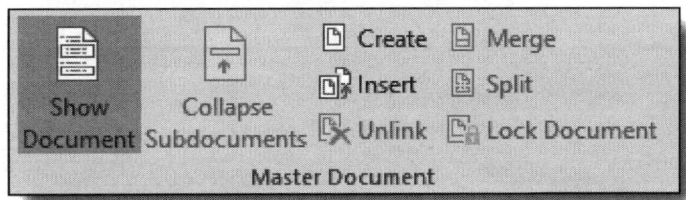

3. Place the cursor where you want to insert the subdocument.
4. Click **Insert**.
5. Browse to the file you want to insert, select it, and click **Open**.

    You can also double-click it.

    The contents of the subdocument are added to the master document.

     Note: It's important to remember that subdocuments cannot be inserted within the body text of the master document. They can be inserted only immediately below a heading.

Organizing subdocuments

There are a number of ways to manipulate subdocuments in a master document.

- To expand or collapse all subdocuments from the Outlining tab, click **Expand Subdocuments** or **Collapse Subdocuments** in the Master Document group.
    It's the same button—the text changes when the subdocuments are expanded or collapsed.

- In Outline view, you can expand and collapse headings that have a plus symbol. Double-click the symbol to expand or collapse the content under that heading.

- To rearrange the order of the subdocuments, on the Outlining tab, with **Show Document** selected and the subdocuments collapsed, you can drag the page icon.
    If you get a message that the document is locked, click the lock symbol and try again.

    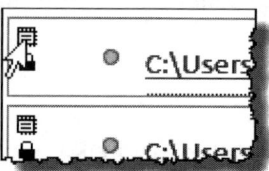

- To reorganize the document outline, expand all the subdocuments and close outline view. Then, on the Headings tab in the Navigation pane, drag headings to a new location.
    Note: If subdocuments are collapsed, the Navigation pane does not see any headings except those in the master document.
    Also note: This effectively allows you to drag content from one subdocument to another, where it is saved if you save the master.

Exercise: Inserting subdocuments

Do This	How & Why
1. Open `Europe`, observe the contents, and close it.	You'll insert this and other documents as subdocuments.
2. Open `History` and save it as `History-master`.	

Do This	How & Why
3. Put the cursor below the last line of text.	You'll insert the first subdocument here. 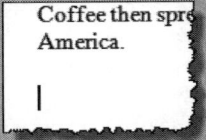
4. On the View tab, click **Outline**.	The Outlining tab appears.
5. On the Outlining tab, click **Show Document**.	
6. Insert the file Europe as a subdocument: a) In the Master Document group, click **Insert**. b) Navigate to the current data folder, and select **Europe**. c) Click **Open**.	The document is inserted in the outline.
7. Repeat the process to Insert `Americas` and `Asia`.	The cursor is already in the right place.
8. Scroll up the document.	You can double-click the white plus signs to collapse or expand headings.
9. Expand all sections, then on the Outlining tab, click **Close Outline View**.	It looks like a continuous document, but its various parts are still stored in separate files. Any changes made here are reflected in those individual files.
10. Press **Ctrl+F**.	To open the Navigation pane. Clear previous search terms, if necessary.
11. In the Navigation pane, on the Headings tab, drag the heading Americas below Indonesia.	This rearranges the document. 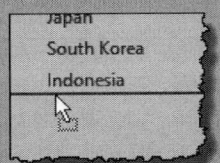 Note that if you drag a heading to another subdocument, that section of text is moved from one file to the other when you save. For instance, if you dragged the England heading under Americas, that section of text is moved to the Americas file on the disk when you save the master document.
12. Save and close the document.	

Assessment: Master documents

1. When you add a subdocument to a master document, the content is copied to the master document, and you no longer need the subdocument.

    - True
    - False

2. How do you turn a document into a master document?

    - Save it as a Master Document file type.
    - On the Insert tab, check Master Document
    - On the Outlining tab, Insert a subdocument.
    - In the Navigation pane, on the Headings tab, click Add Part.

Summary: Navigation and organization

You should now know how to:

- Edit documents with automatic spelling and grammar checking, and with the Spelling and Grammar window; and set proofing, AutoCorrect, and grammar options
- Navigate a large document using the Navigations pane; and use advanced find and replace features, Go To, and the Navigation pane's Search box to find specific document elements
- Use master documents and subdocuments, and rearrange subdocuments

Synthesis: Navigation and organization

1. Open `CoffeeChem` and save it as `CoffeeChem Master`.
2. Switch to Outline view, and add the document `Green Coffee` as a subdocument, at the end.
3. Add more subdocuments, using the files `Artificial Aging`, `Damaged Coffee`, `Acids`, and `Alkaloids`.
4. Switch back to Print Layout view, and open the Navigation pane to the Headings tab.
    Some blank headings might have been added when you inserted subdocuments, and those show up in the Navigation tab.
5. In the Navigation pane, click any blank headings and press the **Delete** key.
    The Navigation pane should show no blank headings.
6. Close the Navigation pane.
7. Save and close the document.

Chapter 6: Saving and sharing documents

You will learn how to:

- Save documents in different file formats and share them with others
- Add and edit comments
- Control who can access or edit a document

Module A: Saving and sending

When you make documents, you probably plan to share them with others. If you're going to print them or save them to a shared folder for other Word users, that's simple enough, but you have many other options to save or distribute them.

You will learn:

- About Word's saving options
- How to save a document in other formats
- How to send documents via the Internet
- How to publish a document as a blog post

Document formats

Word default file format is all you need most of the time, but you can save in a number of other formats, or *file types*, used by other versions of Word or by other programs. Not all file types are interchangeable, though, and some might not support all of Word's features and formatting options. Some don't even support graphics or text formatting.

When you save a document as another file type, it's important to make sure that it's compatible with other users' software, and that it preserves any important information, including formatting, in the document. Whether you simply use **File > Save As** or one of these other options, you end up at the Save As window.

Exam Objective: MOS Word Core 1.5.2

The most common file types you might need are listed in Backstage view, by clicking **Export > Change File Type**. If you've configured Windows to show file extensions, you can tell them apart not only by their icons but by their file extensions.

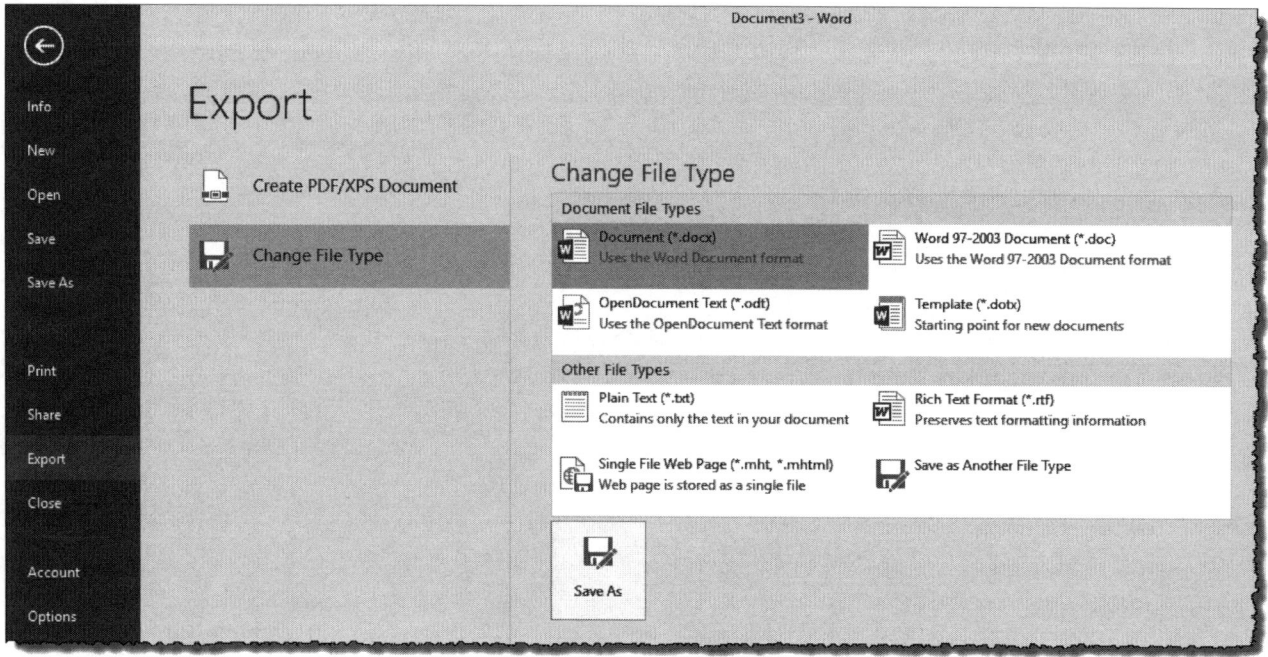

Document (.docx) — The default file format in Word 2007 and later. It supports all of Word's normal functions and is what you should use, unless you have reason not to.

Word 97-2003 Document (.doc) — The file format used by older versions of Word; .doc files are usually larger than .docx files and don't support all of Word's newer features. However, they're more compatible with older software, such as older Office versions.

OpenDocument Text (.odt) — A file format designed by the Organization for the Advancement of Structured Information Standards (OASIS) and used by many non-Microsoft office suites, including OpenOffice. It supports most Word features, but some formatting options might be lost or look different.

Template (.dotx) — The default format for templates in Word 2007 and newer. You shouldn't use this for documents, but instead to make starting points you'll later use to create documents.

Plain Text (.txt) — A simple text file, without any graphics or special formatting. It's the most compatible format, but doesn't save anything other than the text.

Rich Text Format (.rtf) — An older Microsoft format. It preserves basic text formatting information such as font sizes and typefaces, boldface, and italics, but doesn't support most of Word's more advanced features.

Single File Web Page (.mht or .mhtml) — A format meant to be opened by web browsers. Instead of having images, sounds, or other content in separate linked files like a normal web page, this format stores it all in a single easily portable file. It doesn't support all of the same features because it's meant for use by web browsers rather than word processing software.

The other option available in the Export pane is **Create PDF/XPS document**.

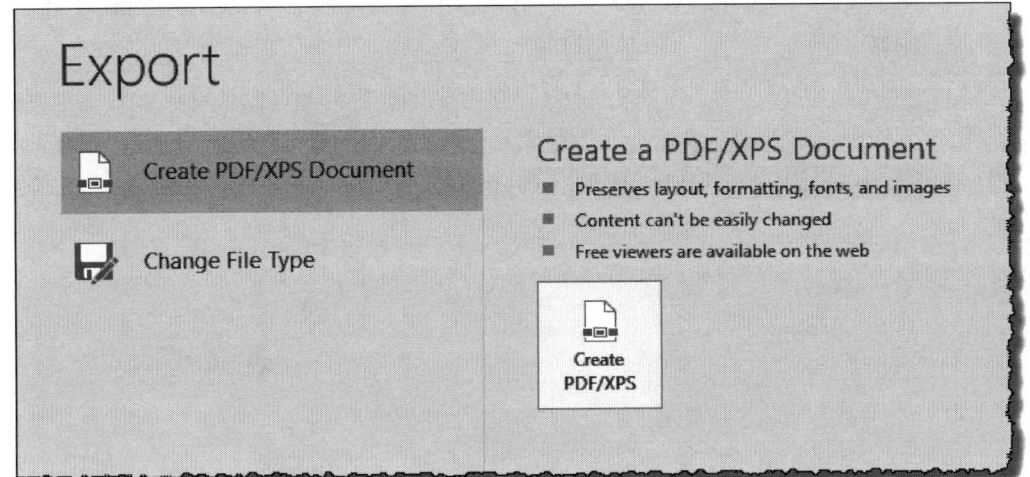

Portable Document Format (.pdf) — Developed by Adobe and broadly supported by many software vendors, PDF was designed to preserve a file's exact formatting and appearance, regardless of viewer or operating system. It is intended for distributing finalized documents, so PDF files really aren't meant to be edited after they're saved. It supports other publication features as well, such as digital signatures and DRM.

XML Paper Specification (.xps) — Microsoft's own equivalent to PDF, XPS has similar features and limitations. It's natively supported by Windows Vista and later as well as other Microsoft products, but is less widely supported by third-party manufacturers.

You can see additional file formats by clicking **Change File Type > Save as Another File Type**, or from the Save As window. These include macro-enabled documents and templates (.docm and .dotm, respectively), web pages (.htm and .html), Word XML documents (.XML), and Microsoft Works 6–9 documents (.wps).

Click **Share** in Backstage view to see options such as emailing your document or posting it to a blog.

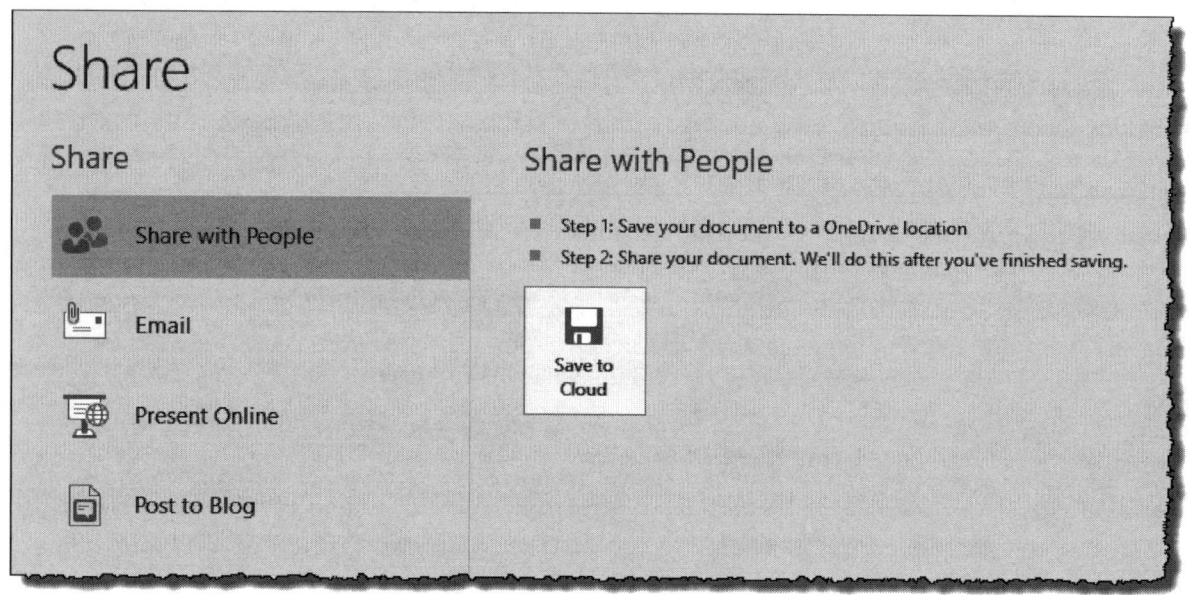

Using Save As options

Exam Objective: MOS Word Core 1.5.2

Whether you're changing a document's file type, saving a newly created file, or just saving a new copy to a different location, you need to use the Save As window. It contains options for file name and location, as well as additional properties, depending on the file type.

The Save As window, when saving a file as a web page.

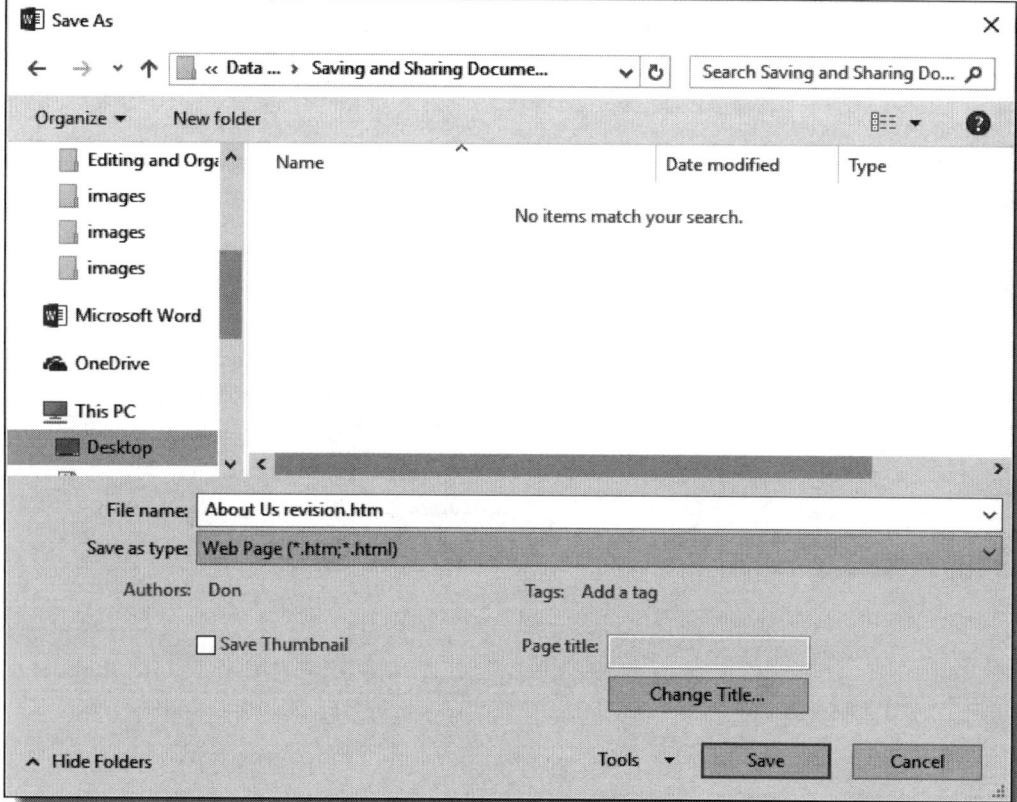

Remember that saving a document with a new name, location, or format doesn't delete the original file. It doesn't update it either. If you want to keep an updated version of the original file, be sure to save it normally before creating the new one. If you don't want to keep it at all, make sure to delete it from Windows Explorer after saving the new file.

1. Open the Save As window.
    - Press **F12**.
    - In Backstage View, click **Save As**, click the main destination location, and click **Browse**. If you select a OneDrive location, you first need to sign in to your account.
    - In Backstage View: click **Export > Change File Type**, select a file type, and click **Save As**; or click **Create PDF/XPS Document > Create PDF/XPS** to open the Publish as PDF or XPS window, another form of the Save As window.
2. Choose the file format from the "Save as type" list. If you used the Export pane, this is already chosen for you.
3. Choose the file's name and location.
    - Navigate through folders using the left pane, or type a file path into the address bar.
    - Enter the file's name, if necessary, in the File Name box.
    Your file type might influence where you want to save it. For example, templates are saved by default in the Templates folder, and you might want to make sure a web page doesn't have any spaces in its file name.
4. Set additional file properties.
    - Many of these vary by file type. For example, web pages have a page title, while PDF documents can be optimized for various publishing methods.
    - Click **Tools** to access additional options, such as file settings or graphics compression.
5. Click **Save**.

For some file types, you'll be asked to specify additional conversion details in a separate window, or you'll receive warnings about compatibility settings.

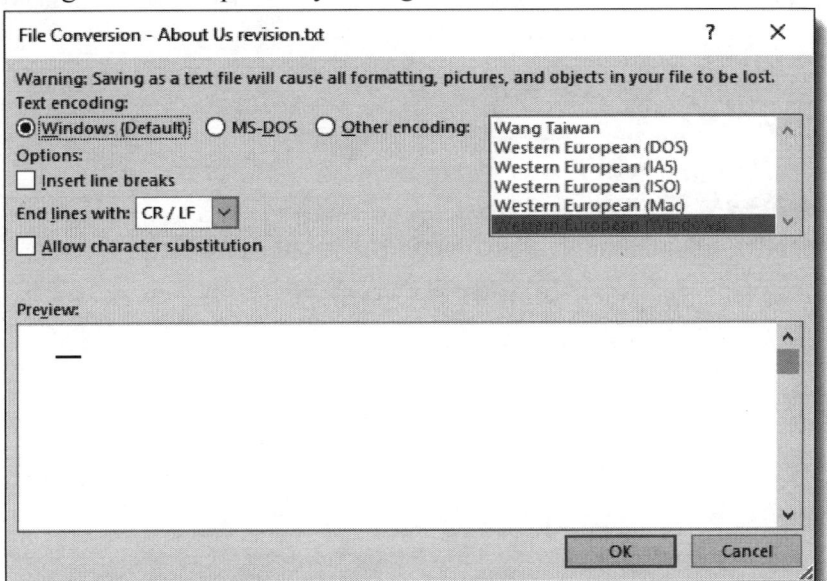

Document properties

Every Word file has various properties automatically associated with it, such as its author, size, the number of pages and words it contains, and the total time it's been edited. In addition, there are other properties that can be edited by you or by any user who has permission to do so. All such document properties as also referred to as its *metadata*.

Exam Objective: MOS Word Core 1.4.5, 1.5.4

- To view and/or edit document metadata, click **File > Info**. The metadata appears under Properties.

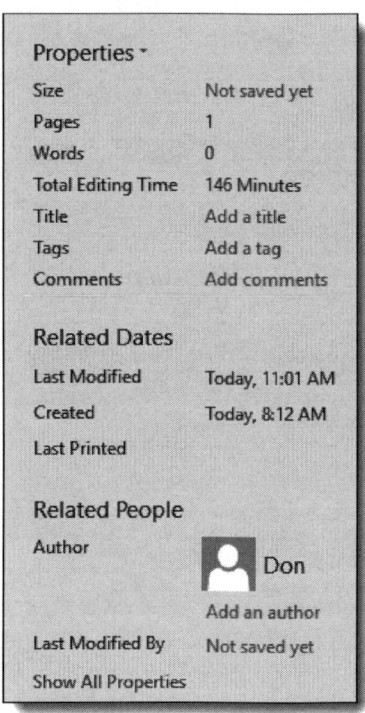

- To add or edit user-defined fields such as Title, Tags, and Comments, click in the field and type.

- To delete user-defined metadata, click in the field, and press **Backspace** or **Delete**.

- To view additional properties/metadata, click **Show All Properties**. Click **Show Fewer Properties** to return to the default setting.

Inspecting a document

When you are sharing a document, especially if you are making it public, you don't want private company or personal information to remain in the metadata. The Document Inspector tool checks for hidden properties and personal information.

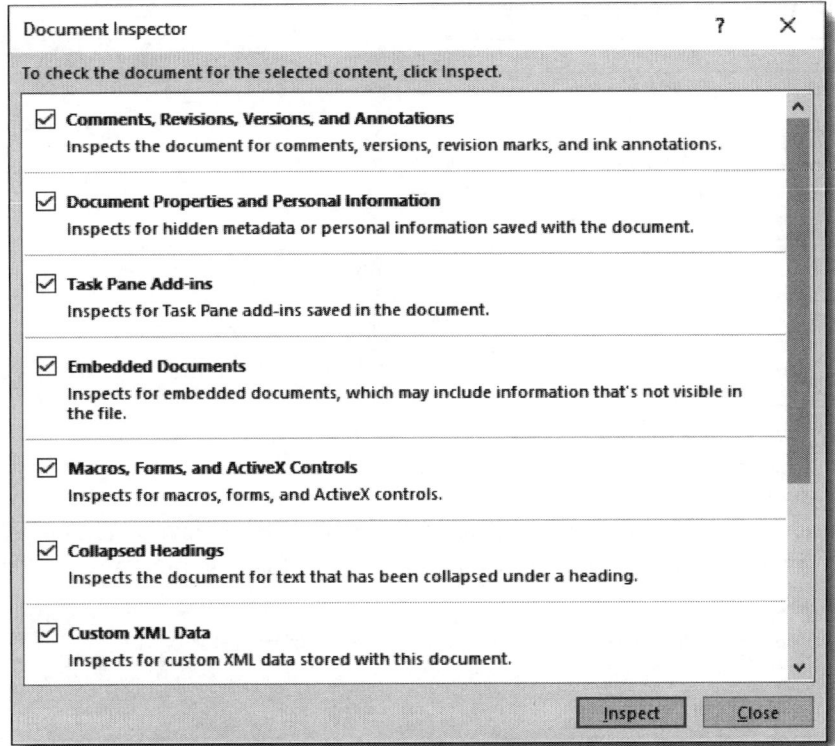

Items the Document Inspector looks for include add-ins, macros, custom XML data, personal information in the properties, and text and other objects that have been formatted to be invisible. The tool allows you to remove this information.

1. In Backstage view, click Info. Then, click **Check for Issues > Inspect Document**.

    The Document Inspector window opens.

2. Check or clear the items you want to look for.
3. Click **Inspect**.

    The inspector highlights possible issues.

4. Click **Remove All** next to any results you wish to remove.
5. Click **Close**.

    You'll still need to save the document to keep these changes.

Creating PDF and XPS documents

PDF and XPS documents are both *fixed formats*, which is to say they're meant to be read but not edited. Both can be read by an assortment of free readers, and all fonts, formatting, and images appear the same on nearly any device. The drawback is that once saved, the content can't be easily changed: think of these formats as a type of printing, even if you can create them as you would any other file type.

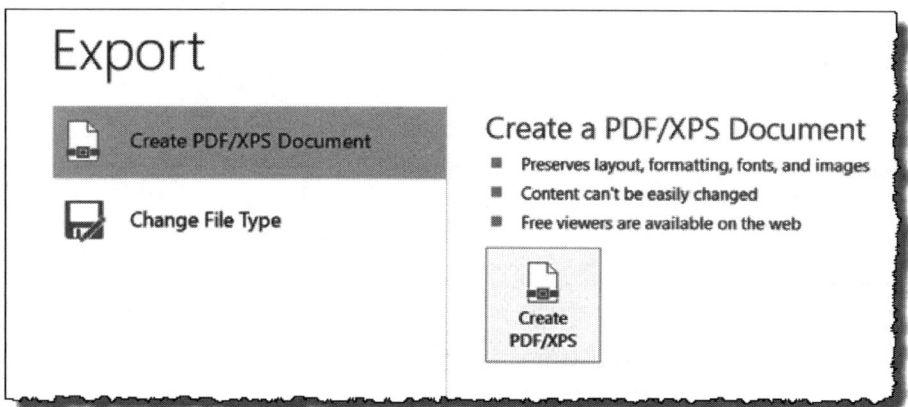

1. Open the Save As window.

   You can also open the nearly identical Publish as PDF or XPS window in Backstage view by clicking **Export > Create PDF/XPS Document > Create PDF/XPS**. The process is otherwise the same.

2. Choose saving options.

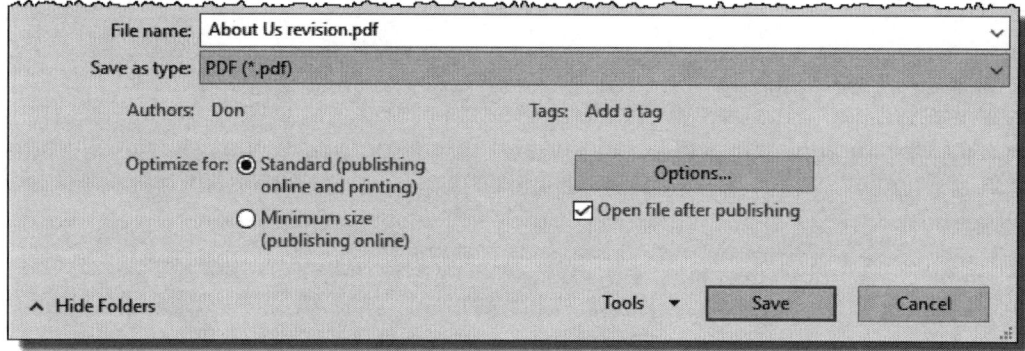

   - Choose either **PDF** or **XPS** from the "Save as type" list.
   - In the Optimize For section, click **Minimum size** to create a smaller file, and **Standard** to preserve graphical quality.
   - Check **Open file after publishing** to automatically open the document in your default PDF or XPS reader.

3. To set additional file options, click **Options**.

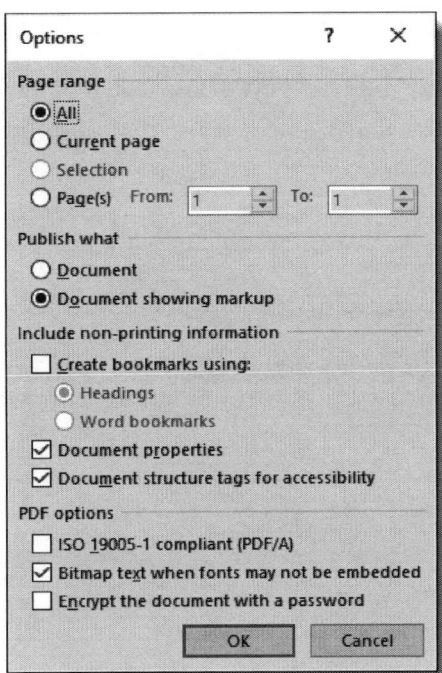

- You can publish the entire document, a page, a page range, or a selection.
- You can optionally include markup, bookmarks, document structure, and document properties.
- PDF and XPS each have additional available options.
- Click **OK** when you're done.

4. Click **Save** or **Publish**.

Importing files

Many types of files can be imported into Word, even those that are non-native to Word, such as those created using Acrobat (PDF), WordPerfect, and OpenOffice.

 Exam Objective: MOS Word Core 1.1.3, 1.1.4

- You can import these files by clicking **File > Open**. At the bottom of the Open window, select the extension associated with the type of file you wish to open. Then select the file, and click **Open**.

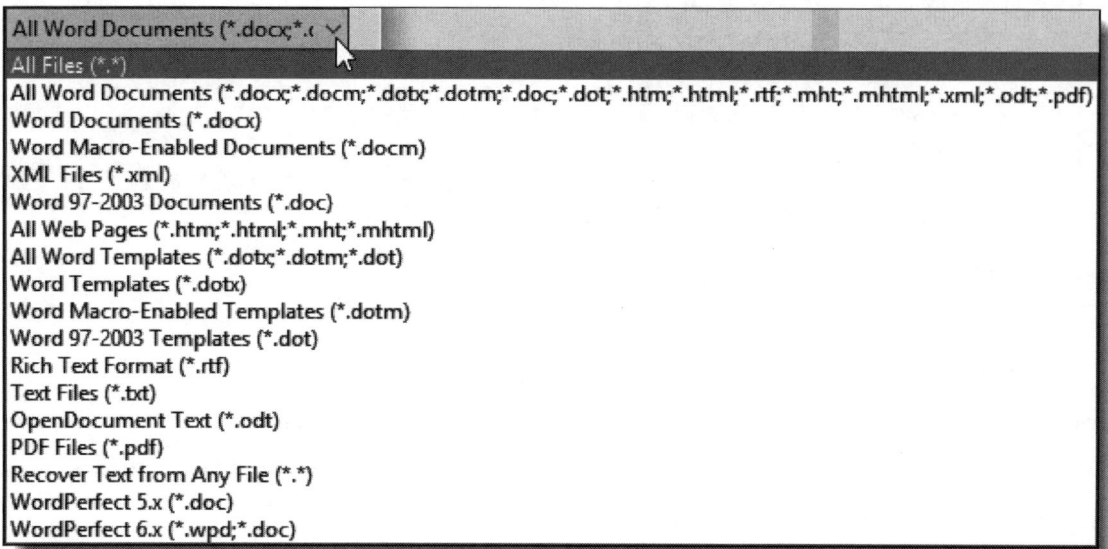

- To append documents directly to a Word document, click **Insert > Object**. In the Object window, click **Create from File**, and click **Browse**. Navigate to the file you want to insert, then click **Insert**. For certain files types, such as portable document format (PDF) files, their contents can't be edited directly in Word; you can only resize it. To edit the PDF, double-click its object to open it in the default PDF reader, then save your changes.

- To insert selected text from a file, click the arrow to the right of the Object button, and select **Text from File**. In the Insert File window, navigate to the file containing the text you wish to insert, and click **Insert**.

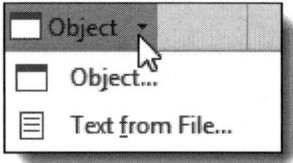

- A quick way to insert text from most types of files is to display the text in its native application, select it, and then copy and paste it into a Word document. Depending on the source of the text, you might be prompted to paste it with its formatting intact or as plain text. However, text copied from some types of files, such as PDFs, can often be pasted only as plain text.

Sending documents

You can attach Word documents to email messages from your mail client as you would any other document, but if you have a compatible mail client like Outlook, you can also send them directly from Word. If you subscribe to an Internet fax service, you can also send a document as a fax message. In addition, if you've saved the file to a shared location, you can send a link to that file. To access these options, in Backstage view, click **Share > Email**.

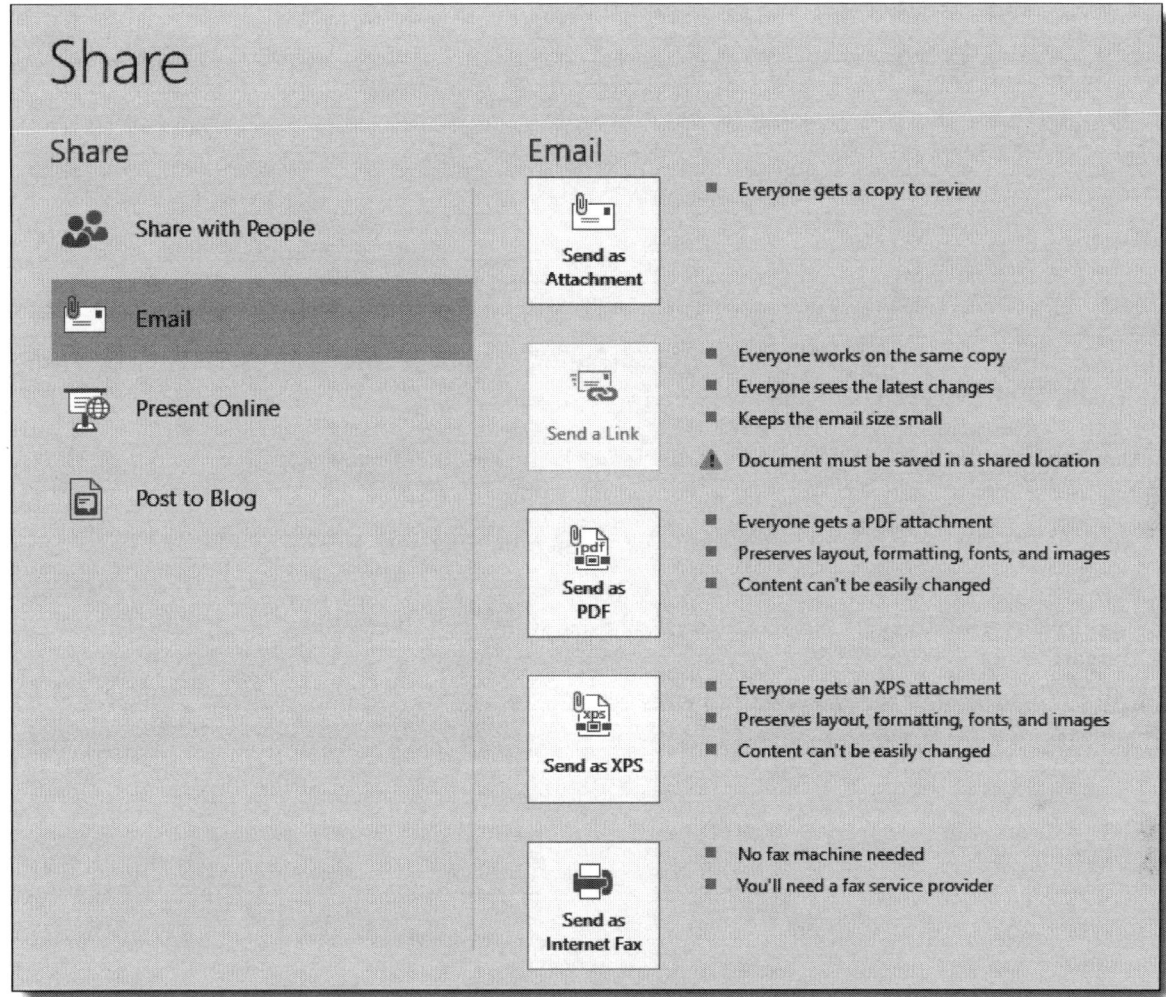

- Click **Send as Attachment** to send the document in its current state and file format.
- Click **Send a Link** to send an email with a hyperlink to the document.
    A link has some advantages over an attachment: it keeps the email size small and ensures the recipients see the original, up-to-date document. The main disadvantage is that you can send a link only if the document is first saved in a shared location the recipient can access.
- Click **Send as PDF** or **Send as XPS** to send a PDF or XPS document using the default save settings.
- Click **Send as Internet Fax** to send the document as a fax. You must be registered with a fax service provider.

Checking accessibility

Exam Objective: MOS Word Core 1.5.5

If you are going to make a document public or distribute it widely, it's good practice to check that the document is accessible to screen readers and other accessibility technology. For instance, pictures should have an alternate text property that describes the picture.

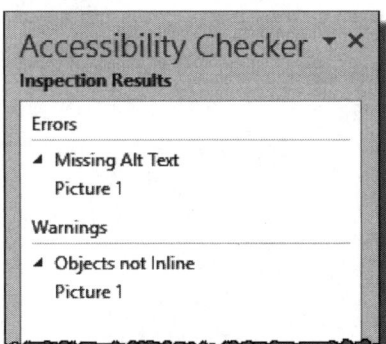

The Accessibility Checker opens as a pane on the right side of the document. It lists possible issues and offers additional information on how to fix them and why you would want to.

1. In Backstage view, in the Info category, click **Check for Issues > Check Accessibility**.

   The Accessibility Checker pane opens, showing results of the inspection.

2. Select an item to see additional information about why you would want to fix the problem and how to do it.

3. If you fix a problem with the pane open, such as adding alternate text to a picture, the results list will update automatically.

4. When you are finished, close the Accessibility Checker pane.

Saving documents to OneDrive

You can also save your documents to cloud storage using online services. If your company uses SharePoint or a OneDrive location, you can save documents to your site from Backstage view by clicking **Save As**, then clicking **OneDrive**, **Office 365 SharePoint**, or another available option. Microsoft's OneDrive service offers cloud storage to anyone with a Microsoft ID. You can create additional destinations in the Save As pane by clicking **Add a Place** and specifying a destination using a Windows SharePoint or other OneDrive location.

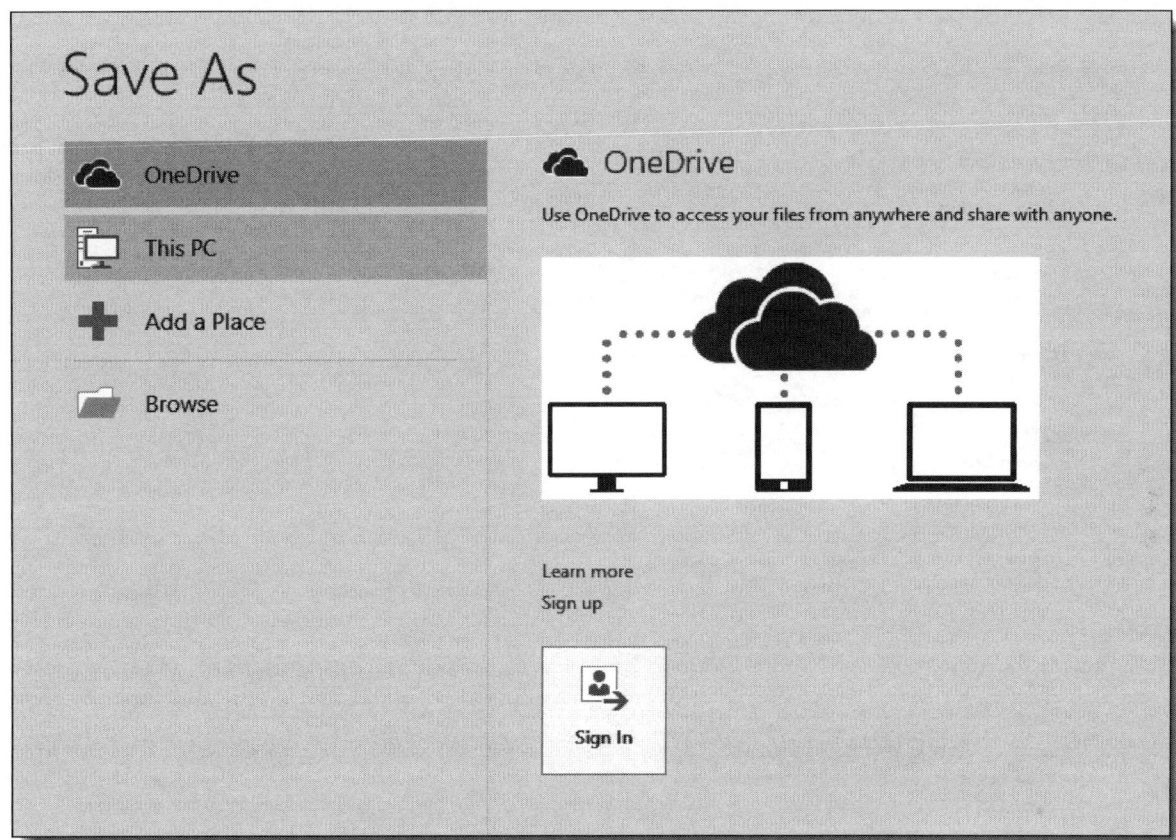

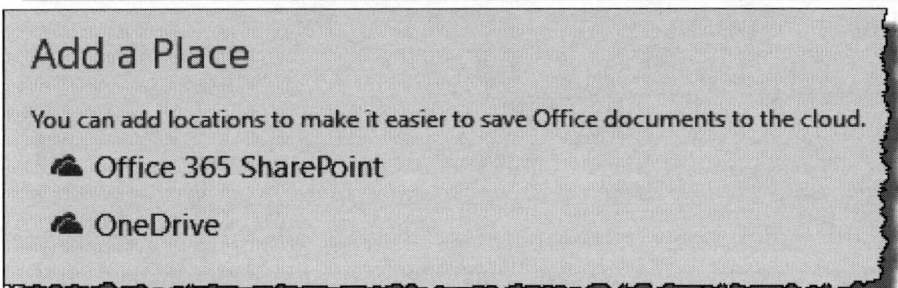

1. In Backstage view, click **Save As > OneDrive**.
2. Click **Sign In**.
3. Enter your Microsoft credentials, and click **OK**.
4. Choose a location in your OneDrive folder.

Registering blog accounts

The first time you create or publish a blog post, you're prompted to register your account in Word.

1. When prompted, click **Register Now**.
2. From the list, select your blog provider.

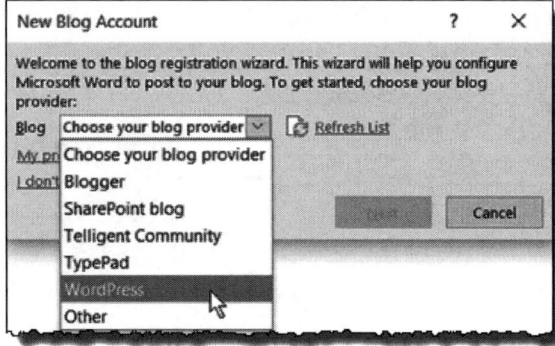

3. Click **Next**.
4. Enter information for your blog.

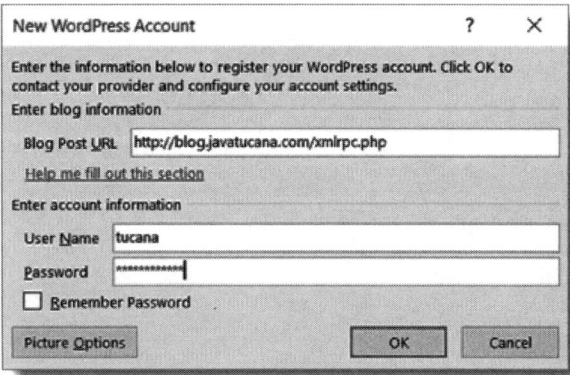

- The fields depend on the service you choose, but at the minimum require a username and password.
- Click **Picture Options** to specify how to handle images used in your blog posts.

5. Click **OK**.

Creating blog posts

You can use Word to create blog posts, but to publish them, you'll need an account with a blog service.

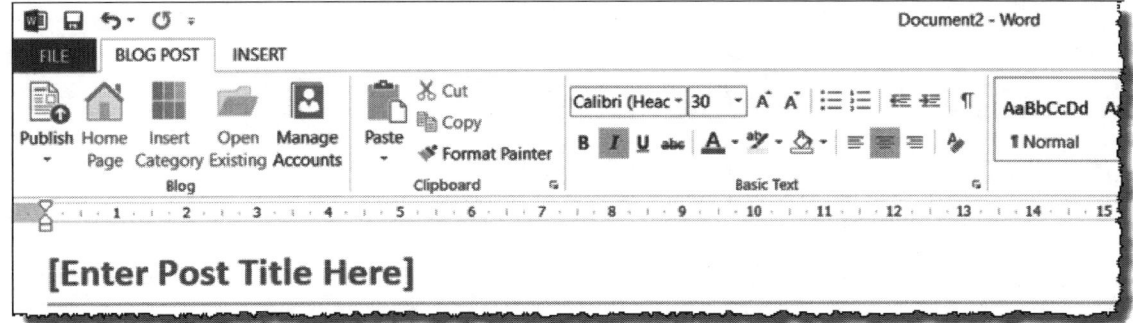

- To create a new blog post, click **New** in Backstage view, select the Blog post template, and click **Create**.
- To publish an existing document as a blog post, in Backstage view, click **Share > Post to Blog > Post to Blog**. If you haven't yet registered with a blog service, you'll be prompted to do so.
- When you're editing a blog post, you have access to the Blog Post tab of the ribbon, with formatting and publishing options.

Viewing shared documents

When you open a document someone else has sent to you, you might see a notification that Word is operating in *Compatibility Mode* or *Protected View*.

 Exam Objective: MOS Word Core 1.5.6

- When you open a document in a format that doesn't support all of Word 2016's features, "Compatibility Mode" appears next to the file name at the top of the window. Word may disable any features not compatible with the document type. To leave Compatibility Mode, save the document in .docx format.

- To maintain "backward" compatibility with earlier versions of Word, so that others using those versions can open and work with your files, select the appropriate Word version in the "Save as type" list of the Save As window.
- When "Protected View" appears in the document title, it means that Word thinks your document might pose a security risk. Most ribbon commands are disabled, and although you can view or copy document content, you can't edit it. A message bar also appears, explaining the reason. If you trust the document's security, click **Enable Editing** to leave Protected view.

 Note: "Protected View" doesn't necessarily mean a file is dangerous: it usually just means it came from the Internet or some other potentially unsafe location. At the same time, if you don't know and trust a file's sender, don't leave Protected View until you make sure it's safe, for example, by scanning it with an antivirus program.

Checking compatibility

If you want to save a document to an earlier Word format, you can first use the compatibility checker to see if your document uses features that are not supported in earlier versions of Word.

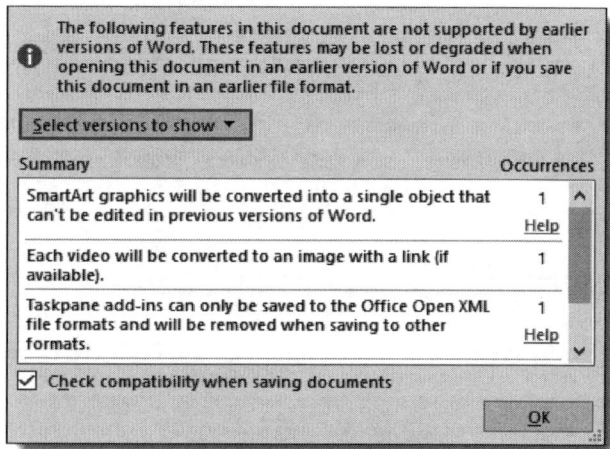

Compatibility issues include things like SmartArt and WordArt, some chart features, embedded online videos, new numbering formats and new shapes, add-ins, and several more. By default, compatibility is checked whenever you save a document to an earlier version of Word, but you can check it at any time.

1. In Backstage view, in the Info category, click **Check for Issues > Check Compatibility**.

    The Compatibility Checker window opens. Each issue is summarized with the number of occurrences in the document.

2. If you want to check compatibility with a specific Word version, you can select only that version in the "Select versions to show" list.

    By default, the document is checked against Word 97-2003, 2007, and 2010. There are no compatibility issues between Word 2013 and 2016.

3. Click **OK** to close the Compatibility Checker.

Exercise: Exploring file types

To complete this exercise, you need to have Adobe Reader installed. If you don't, and are using Windows Vista or newer, you can save as XPS instead of PDF. You'll save a document in different file types.

Do This	How & Why
1. Open `Lunch menu`.	This file is an ordinary Word document. You'll save it in other formats.
2. Save the file in OpenDocument format.	You need to make a copy of the file for someone who uses OpenOffice.
a) In Backstage view, click **Export**.	To view the available options. You want to save it as a different file type.
b) Click **Change File Type**.	

Do This	How & Why
c) In the right pane, click **OpenDocument Text**.	

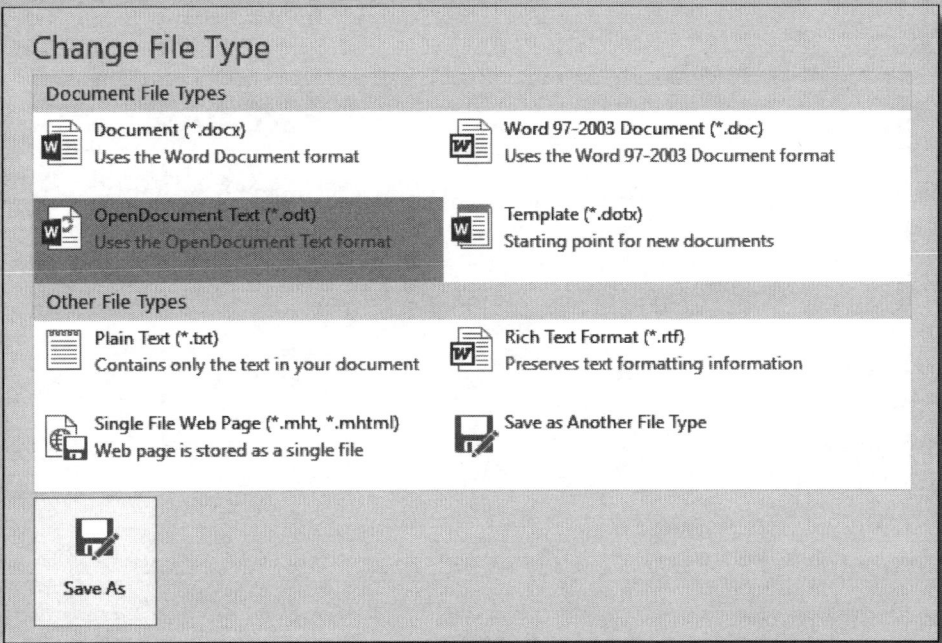

Do This	How & Why
d) Click **Save As**.	The Save As window opens. OpenDocument Text is already selected in the "Save as type" list.
e) Save the file as `Lunch menu export`.	Type the file name, and click **Save**. You are warned that the new format might not support all the features of the Word format.
f) Click **Yes**.	

To close the warning and save the document as an odt file.

The file is now shown as OpenDocument Text (odt). Because this file doesn't use any different features, it doesn't look any different, and it can be opened by OpenOffice Writer and other programs.

Do This	How & Why
3. Save the document in PDF format.	The commercial printer making your menus prefers a fixed format to avoid any layout problems, so you'll use PDF.
a) Press **F12**.	The Save As window opens. You don't need to use Backstage view to change file types.
b) From the "Save as type" list, Choose **PDF**.	Additional options specific to PDF appear. The optimization setting is set to Standard, which is what you want.
c) Click **Options**.	The Options window opens. You'll print the whole document, and you don't need markup or bookmarks, so you'll keep these options.

Do This	How & Why
d) Click **OK**.	To close the window.
e) Check **Open File After Publishing**.	
f) Specify `Lunch menu portable` as the file name.	
g) Click **Save**.	You may need to accept the Adobe Acrobat Reader license. The PDF opens in Adobe Acrobat Reader. It looks the same, but you can't edit it.
h) Close Acrobat Reader.	**Lunch menu compatibility** is still open in Word.
4. Explore other saving options.	
a) In Backstage view, click **Share**.	You can send the document as an attachment, a link, a PDF or XPS document, or an Internet Fax.
b) Click **Invite People**, which displays the **Save To Cloud** option in the right pane.	You can log into your Microsoft account and save the document to your OneDrive folder.
c) Click **Save to SharePoint**.	To save the file to your team's SharePoint site.
d) Click **Post to Blog**. In the right pane, click **Post to Blog**.	
	The document opens in a new window as a blog post. The page color and border are no longer visible, and the Blog Post tab is active on the ribbon. Additionally, the Register a Blog Account window opens.
e) Click **Register Now**.	The New Blog Account window opens. You can connect Word to your existing blog account from here.
f) Click **Cancel**.	The New Blog Account window closes, but you're still editing the file as a blog post.
5. Close the new document window.	Don't save changes.
6. Save and close `Lunch menu export`.	

The lunch menu displayed as a blog post.

[Enter Post Title Here]

JAVA TUCANA

LUNCH MENU

POLLO CRAZIN $6

Chicken salad with dried cranberries on a ciabatta roll.

TURKRAN SAN $6

A meal on a bun! Turkey, cranberry, and stuffing on a grilled panini roll.

WALDORF HYSTERIA $5

Boston lettuce, apple, walnuts, and raisins with a mayo-yogurt dressing rolled in a spinach

Assessment: Saving and sending

Checking knowledge about saving and sending files.

1. You need a colleague to edit a rather complex document, but his non-Microsoft word processing application can't reliably read Word's default format. What format would preserve most of your current formatting options while still being readable to the other application?

    - OpenDocument Text
    - PDF
    - Rich Text Format
    - XPS

2. XPS is natively supported by Windows Vista and later. True or false?

    - True
    - False

3. Word is really compatible only with blogs using Microsoft's Windows Live Spaces format. True or false?

    - True
    - False

4. What should you do if Word opens a document in Protected view? Choose the best response.

    - Continue as normal: Protected view lets you edit the document safely.
    - Delete or quarantine the file: Word has detected malware in it, and it's unsafe to open.
    - **Disable Protected view if you trust the document's source.**
    - Save the document in the default .docx format.

Module B: Comments

When you're working on a document with other people, you might want to make comments or add reminders for later. You could just add them in the text and remove them later, but they might be hard to spot or get left in by mistake. Instead, Word lets you add comments as markup, rather than as document content.

You will learn how to:

- Insert comments
- Edit comments
- Change comment display options

About comments

By default, comments appear as balloons in the document margin, but the comment text doesn't print. You can display hidden comments clicking the comment balloon, or from the Review tab by clicking **Show Comments**. When you hover over or click on a comment balloon, the document text to which it refers is also highlighted for convenience.

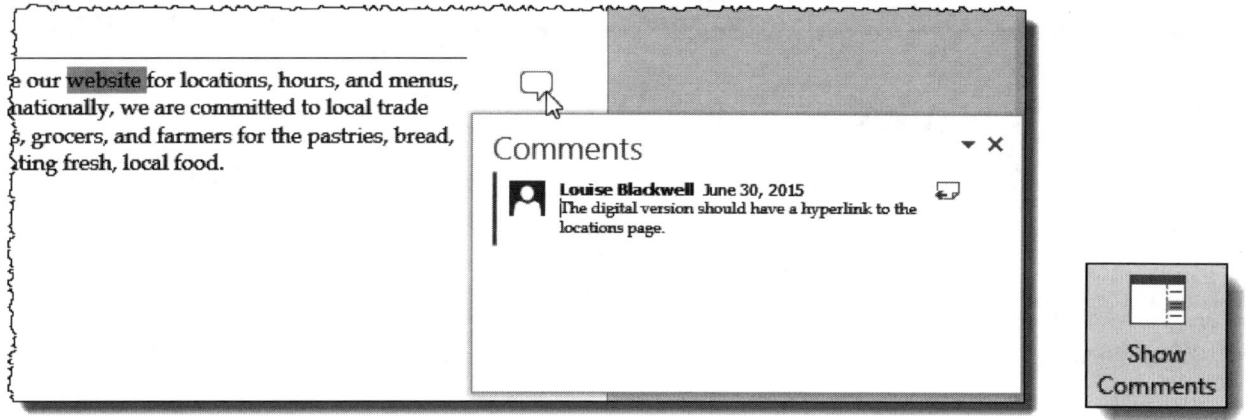

A comment is always marked with the name of the user who created it, and when a document has comments from multiple users, they're color coded. If one comment is in response to another, it will appear in the same window.

Exam Objective: MOS Word Expert 1.3.1, 1.3.2

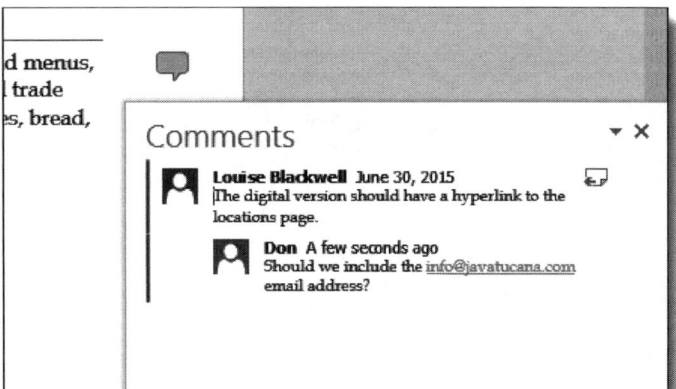

Commands for managing comments are located on the Review tab, in the Comments group. The Ink Comment options allow you to write comments by using a touch screen, the mouse, or another pointer as a pen.

Adding comments

 Exam Objective: MOS Word Expert 1.3.4

When you add a comment, it is attached to any content that is selected or the word nearest the cursor if no content is selected. When you're commenting on something like a sentence or graphic, this helps point it out. If you want to make a general comment about the document, you can place it wherever you like.

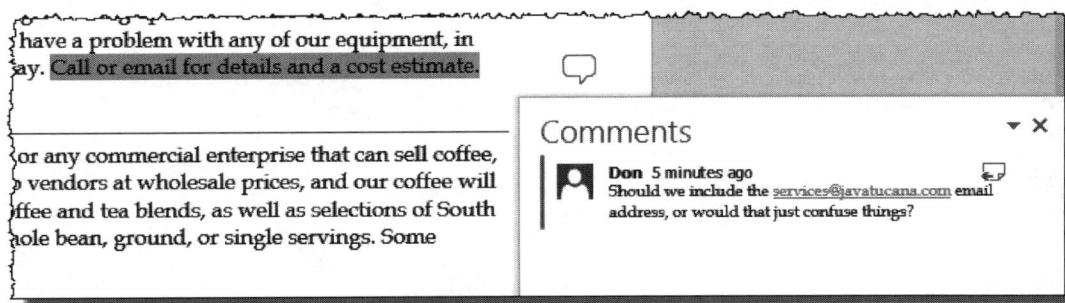

1. Place the insertion point or make a selection.
   - If you make a selection, the comment points to the whole selection.
   - If you merely place the insertion point, the comment points to the nearest word.
2. In the Comments group, click **New Comment**.
3. Write the comment.

    Note: Usually, you need to make comments only as plain text, but you can apply some formatting, like changing font type, and even insert images. However, you can't change text size or paragraph formatting.

4. Click outside the comment box when you're done writing it.

Managing comments

You can edit or delete existing comments. You can also navigate easily through all comments of a long document.

 Exam Objective: MOS Word Expert 1.3.4, 1.3.5

- To edit a comment, click anywhere in its text, and make any changes you like.
- To delete a comment, select it, and click **Delete** in the Comments group.
  - To delete all visible comments, click **Delete > Delete All Comments Shown**.
  - To delete all comments, click **Delete > Delete All Comments in Document**.
- To navigate between comments, click **Next** or **Previous**.

Displaying comments

You might not always want to display comments as balloons—or even at all—especially if you want to print a copy of the document without the comments. You can change how comments are displayed on the Review tab, in the tracking group. Most of those options are also in the **Show Markup** menu.

 Exam Objective: MOS Word Expert 1.3.4, 1.3.5

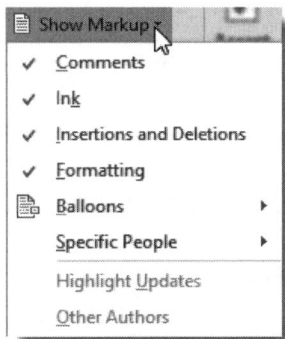

- To display or hide all comments, click **Show Markup** > **Comments**. Or, you can click **Show Comments** in the Comments group, when it's available (in other words, not dimmed).

- To display or hide comments from a specific user, click **Show Markup** > **Specific People**, and check or clear **All Reviewers** or individual users' names.

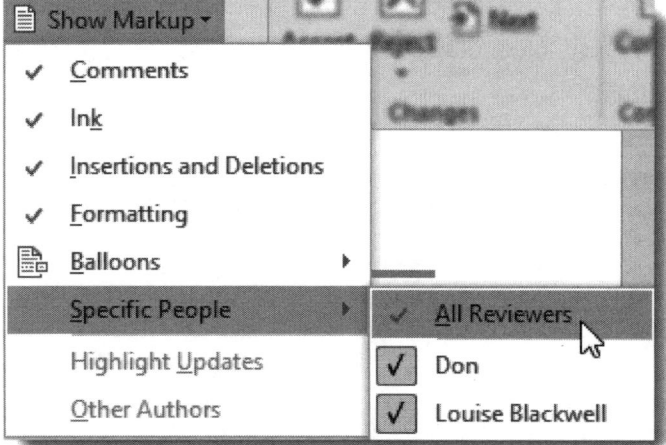

- To show comments without balloons, click **Show Markup** > **Balloons** > **Show All Revisions Inline**

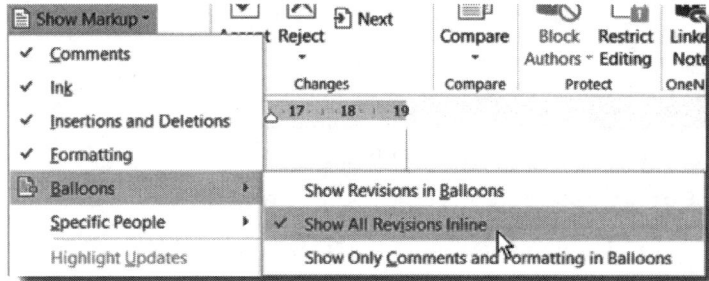

- To view further information about a comment, balloon or line, click it.

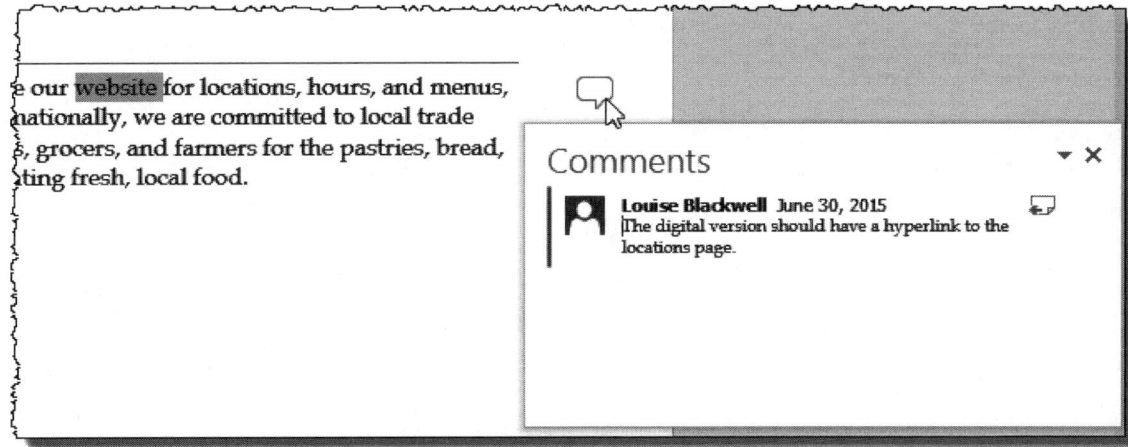

- Click **Reviewing Pane** to show all visible comments in a separate pane.

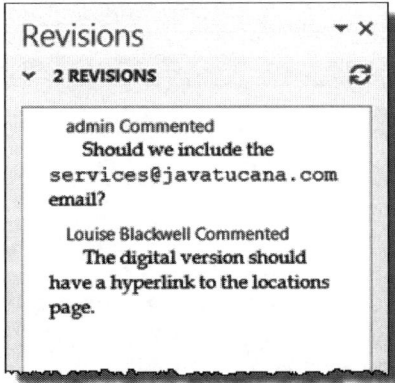

Exercise: Commenting on a document

In this exercise, you'll use comments to review a document.

Do This	How & Why
1. Open `About Us revision`, and save it as `About Us comments`.	This document already has one comment from a coworker.
2. Point to the word "website" in the document.	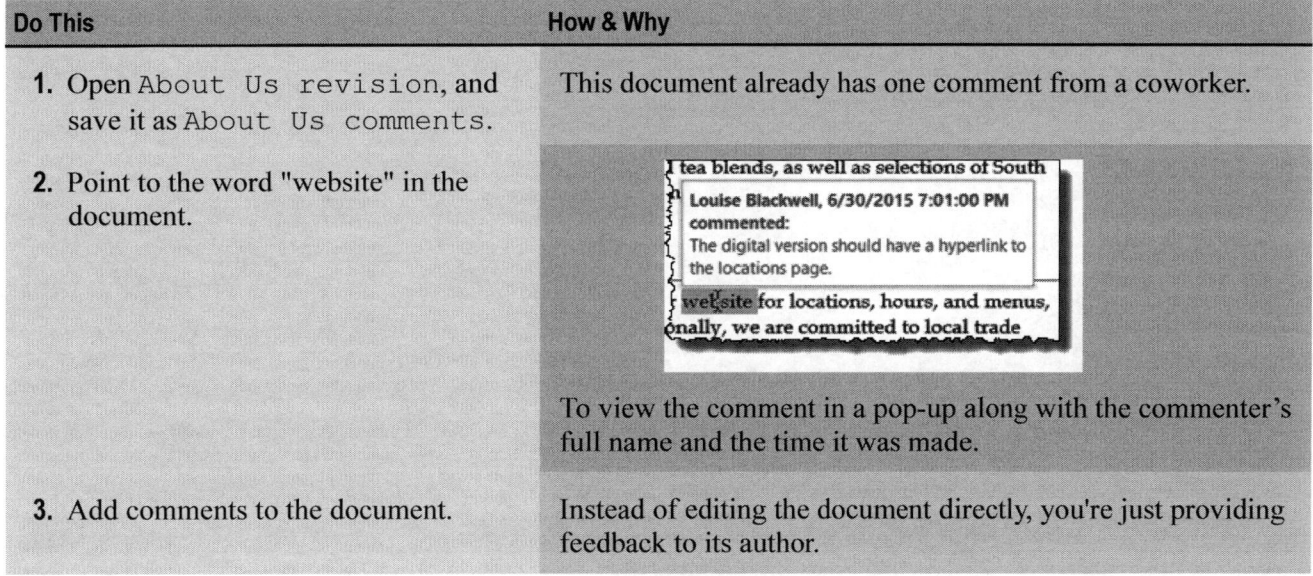 To view the comment in a pop-up along with the commenter's full name and the time it was made.
3. Add comments to the document.	Instead of editing the document directly, you're just providing feedback to its author.

Word 2016 Level 2 143

Do This	How & Why
a) Select the logo at the top of the document.	
b) On the Review tab, click **New Comment**.	A blank comment balloon appears in the right margin. It shows your name or initials and is a different color than the existing comment.
c) Type `Be sure to use the newest version of the logo.`	
d) Select the last sentence of the "Office coffee service" paragraph.	"Call or email for details and a cost estimate."
e) Comment `Should we include the Office coffee services email?`	Click **New Comment**, and type it.
f) Click outside the comment box.	To deselect it. The whole sentence you selected is highlighted as the target of the comment.

4. Edit your comments.

a) Click the comment you just made.	You'll include the email address.
b) In the comment, Select "Office coffee services."	
c) Type `services@javatucana.com`.	You can edit a comment just as you would any other text.
d) In the Comments group, click **Previous**.	To move to the first comment. You've learned this is the newest logo after all, so you'll delete the comment.
e) In the comments group, click **Delete**.	
	The comment is deleted.

Do This	How & Why
5. Change comment display options.	
a) In the Markup group, click **Show Markup > Balloons > Show All Revisions Inline**	The balloons in the margin vanish. Now each comment is just a colored highlight with initials and a number.
b) Point to any comment.	The comment's full content appears as a pop-up.
c) Click **Show Markup > Balloons > Show Only Comments and Formatting in Balloons**.	To return to the default view.
d) Click **Show Markup > Comments**	To hide all comments. Now you can print the document without the comments showing.
6. Save and close the document.	

Assessment: Comments

Checking knowledge about comments.

1. What can you do when editing a comment? Choose all that apply.
   - Adjust paragraph settings
   - Change character size
   - Change the font
   - Insert an image

2. If you want to print a document without showing comments, you have to delete them all. True or false?
   - True
   - False

3. To view an inline comment's full content, you need to show balloons or the Reviewing Pane. True or false?
   - True
   - False

Module C: Protecting documents

When you distribute a document, you might want to restrict who uses it or what they can do with it. Word allows you to control who can open a document, specify what kinds of changes they can make, and even make sure the document isn't changed without your knowledge.

You will learn:

- About Word's protection options
- How to mark a document as final
- How to password-protect a document
- How to restrict document editing

Document protection options

All document protection options are available in the Info section of Backstage view. Each option has a different purpose, and some can even be used together, so it's important to understand the features and limitations of each.

Exam Objective: MOS Word Expert 1.2.1, 1.2.2, 1.2.3

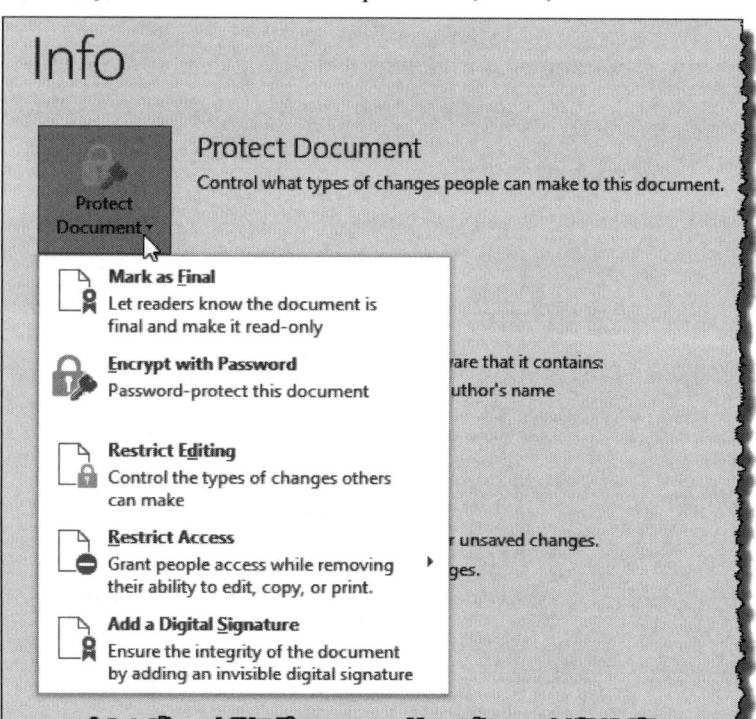

Mark as Final	Makes a document read-only and marks its status as final. This isn't a security feature: it just records your finalization of the document and keeps it from being changed by accident.
Encrypt with Password	Applies encryption to the document using a password of your choice. No one can open or read the document without the password.
Restrict Editing	Allows anyone to read the document, but controls what they can change about it. In addition to preventing all changes, you can just restrict users to using a fixed set of styles, to making tracked changes or comments, or to filling in forms.

Restrict Access Grants access to the document using Microsoft's Information Rights Management Service. This gives you broad abilities to restrict who can open the document and what they can do with it, but you must install the free service, and you and all users must have Microsoft IDs.

Add a Digital Signature Applies a visible or invisible cryptographic signature to the document, proving that it is from you and hasn't been altered. You can apply your own digital signature, but the full benefits of the feature require a third-party signature verification service.

Marking documents final

When you mark a document as final, Word makes it read-only and saves it as it is. When you or another user opens the document, the ribbon is minimized, all editing and proofing functions are disabled, and a Marked as Final message bar is shown at the top of the window. This doesn't actually provide any security for the document: you or anyone else can simply remove the mark and edit it again.

 Exam Objective: MOS Word Expert 1.2.2

1. In the Info section of Backstage view, click **Protect Document** > **Mark as Final**.
   You are asked to confirm the change.
2. Click **OK**.
   When you first use this feature, an additional notification window appears, explaining finalized documents. You can choose not to receive this notice in the future.

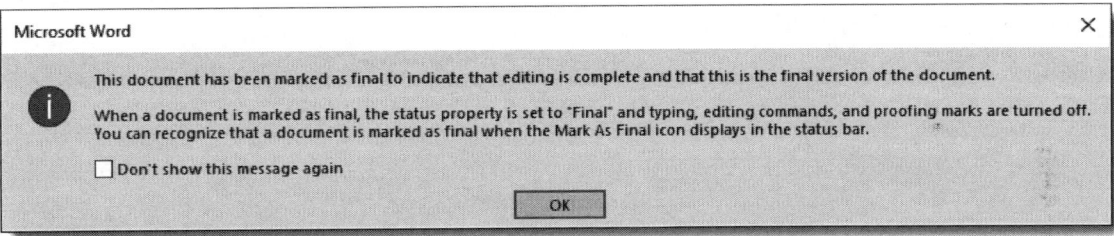

After you mark a document as final, it remains open. Because it's saved as part of the process, you can just close it without further action.

Password-encrypting documents

You encrypt a document with a password when you want to make sure unauthorized users can't read it but don't want to deal with a more involved user-based security system.

 Exam Objective: MOS Word Expert 1.2.3

When you open a password-protected document, you're prompted to enter the password. If you don't, the document won't open at all. If you do, you are free to make any changes you want, including removing the password.

Note: Earlier versions of Word used weak encryption methods that could easily be defeated. The encryption used by Word 2007 and later is much improved and is suitable for protecting sensitive data when used correctly. Keep the following in mind when encrypting a document.

- Choose a password that is long and hard to guess. A simple password will never be secure, regardless of the encryption method.
- Passwords are case-sensitive, so be mindful when you create them.
- There is no password recovery feature for encrypted documents. If you forget the password for your document, there is no Word option or Microsoft service to easily retrieve your data.

1. In the Info section of Backstage view, click **Protect Document > Encrypt with Password**.
    You're prompted to create a password.

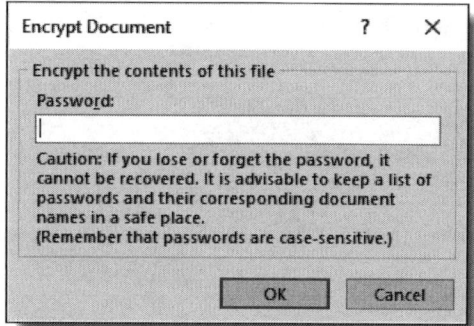

2. Enter the password you want, and click **OK**.
    To remove the password from a document that's already encrypted, delete the existing password and then click **OK**. You're prompted to re-enter the password.

3. Type the password again, then click **OK**.

Unlike finalized documents, encrypted documents aren't automatically saved, so you still need to save before closing.

Document restrictions

When you apply restrictions to a document, anyone can open and read it, but you can control what kind of changes they can make, if any. Editing protections are handled through the Restrict Formatting and Editing pane. When you apply protection to a document, the pane shows options for what you can restrict. Once protections are enabled, the pane instead shows you what changes you can make.

 Exam Objective: MOS Word Expert 1.2.1

The Restrict Formatting and Editing pane before and after applying editing restrictions.

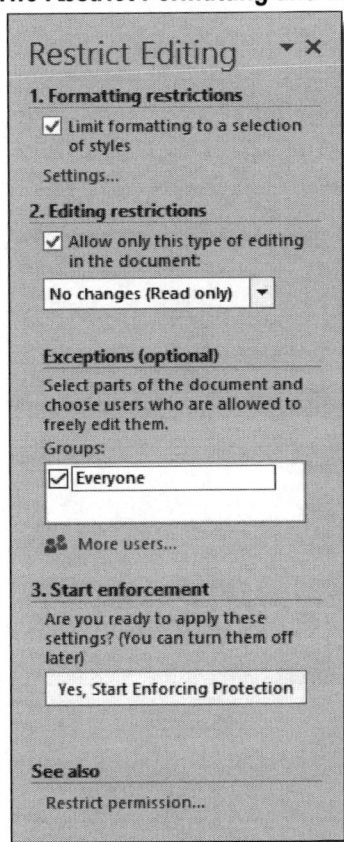
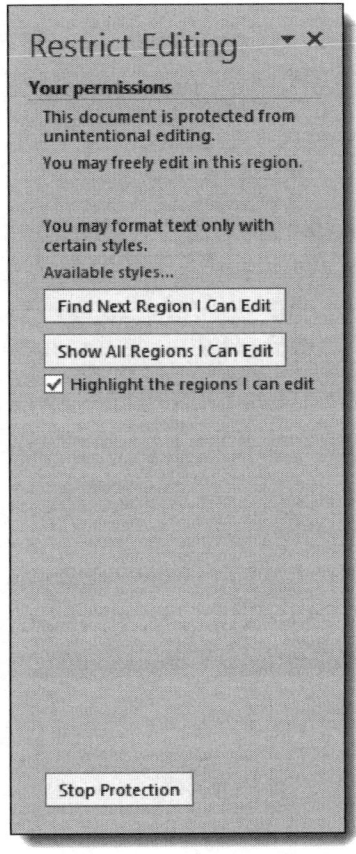

You can apply three main kinds of editing restrictions.

Formatting restrictions Control what changes users can make to document formatting. You can prevent users from applying manual formatting, restrict the styles they can use, and even prevent them from changing the document theme or style set.

Editing restrictions Control what changes users can make to the document's content. In addition to simply making the document read-only, you can restrict users to making only tracked changes or comments, or to filling in forms.

Exceptions Mark areas of the document that aren't protected and can be edited freely. You can set exceptions only if you've set editing restrictions to prevent all changes, or allow comments only.

When document protection is enforced, it applies until it's removed. If you just want to keep a document from being edited by accident, you can enforce protection without authentication so anyone can turn it off. You can also require a password to remove document protection or restrict it to certain users, if you're using Information Rights Management.

 Note: Don't confuse document protection with document encryption. If you're using user authentication through Windows Live IDs, the document is both protected and encrypted. If you're using passwords, they are separate. You can apply protection, encryption, or both, each with its own password.

Applying document restrictions

To apply protection to a document, you have to set restrictions, then start enforcement.

 Exam Objective: MOS Word Expert 1.2.1

1. Open the Restrict Editing pane. You can do this two ways.
   - From Backstage view, click **Info > Protect Document > Restrict Editing**.
   - On the ribbon's Review tab, in the Protect group, click **Restrict Editing**.

2. Choose restrictions.
   - To set formatting restrictions, check **Limit formatting to a selection of styles**, or click **Settings** for finer control.
   - To set editing restrictions, check **Allow only this type of editing in the document**, then select an option from the list: Tracked Changes, Comments, Filling in forms, or No Changes.
   - To set an exception, select the portion of the document you want to be editable, and in the Exceptions list, check **Everyone**.

3. Click **Yes, Start Enforcing Protection**.

4. Choose enforcement options.
   - To protect the document using Information Rights Management, choose **User Authentication**.
   - To protect editing restrictions with a password, enter it in both fields.
   - To enforce restrictions without a password, leave both fields blank.

5. Click **OK**.

Editing restricted documents

When you open a protected document, you can make only whatever changes the current protection allows. The Restrict Editing pane shows further details and commands to help you.

- You can use any available commands on the ribbon; restricted commands are simply made unavailable.
- If the document is locked to allow only you to fill out form fields, you will be able to select only those fields. Otherwise, you can click in or select any part of the document, even if you can't edit it.
- By default, exceptions in the document are highlighted. To find exceptions, click **Find Next Region I Can Edit** or **Show All Regions I Can Edit**.
- Click **Stop Protection** to turn off all protection, if you have the necessary credentials.

Exercise: Using protection features

In this exercise, you'll apply various protection types to multiple documents.

Do This	How & Why
1. Open `Lunch menu` and save it as `Lunch menu protected`.	
2. Encrypt the document.	First, you'll apply password encryption to restrict who can open the menu until it's ready for circulation.
a) In Backstage view, click **Info > Protect Document > Encrypt with Password**.	The Encrypt Document window appears.
b) Type `password` and click **OK**.	For a real document, you'd want to use a stronger password. You're prompted to confirm the password.
c) Enter the `password` again.	Type `password` and click **OK**. The document now requires a password to be opened.
3. Mark the document as final.	You can apply more than one kind of protection to the same document. In this case, you just want to make sure that anyone who opens the document knows it's the final version.
a) Click **Protect Document > Mark as Final**.	A confirmation window appears, asking if you want to proceed.
b) Click **OK**.	An information window appears, explaining finalized documents.
c) Click **OK**.	
d) Close the document.	You aren't prompted to save changes, as finalizing the document saved it automatically.
4. Remove the document's protection.	

Do This	How & Why
a) Open `Lunch menu protected`.	You're prompted for a password.
b) Enter `password` and click **OK**.	You can read the document, but the ribbon is minimized, the document's title states that it's read-only, and a message bar explains that it has been marked as final.
c) Try to edit the document.	You can select document content but not modify it.
d) In the message bar, click **Edit Anyway**.	The message bar vanishes, and the ribbon is displayed.
e) In Backstage view, click **Info > Protect Document > Encrypt with Password**.	The Encrypt Document window opens. The current password is shown as dots.
f) Delete the document password, and click **OK**.	To remove the password. The document's permissions are now open.
g) Save and close the document.	
5. Open `Office services` and save it as `Office services protected`.	This document is a form.
6. Restrict editing of the document.	You'll restrict it so users can fill out the form but not make other changes.
a) On the Review tab, click **Restrict Editing**.	The Restrict Editing pane appears.
b) Check **Allow only this type of editing in the document**.	By default, No changes (Read only) is selected. That isn't what you want.
c) From the Editing restrictions list, choose **Filling in forms**.	
d) Click **Yes, Start Enforcing Protection**.	The Start Enforcing Protection window appears. Password is selected.

Do This	How & Why
e) In both password fields, type `12345`. f) Click **OK**.	If you just wanted to protect against accidental edits, you wouldn't need to use a password. **Restrict Editing** **Your permissions** This document is protected from unintentional editing. You may only fill in forms in this region.
g) Close the Restrict Editing pane.	
7. Fill out the form.	You can edit form fields, but you can't even select other parts of the document.
8. Save and close the document.	

Assessment: Protecting documents

Checking knowledge about document protection.

1. When you mark a document as final, you can specify a password needed to unlock it for editing. True or false?
   - True
   - False

2. For technical reasons, document encryption and editing restrictions don't work well together. True or false?
   - True
   - False

3. It's easy to recognize exceptions in a restricted document. True or false?
   - True
   - False

4. If you forget a document's encryption password, there's no easy way to recover it. True or false?
   - True
   - False

Summary: Saving and sharing documents

You should now know how to:

- Save documents in other file formats, publish them to fixed formats, and distribute them to others over the Internet
- Add, remove, and edit comments in a document
- Mark a document as final, encrypt its contents, or restrict how users can edit it

Synthesis: Saving and sharing documents

Bringing together your knowledge of sharing and collaboration.

In this document, you'll use saving and sharing features.

1. Open `Franchise information`, and save it as `Franchise information sharing`.
2. Apply protection to the document.
   - Encrypt the document using one password, and restrict editing using a different password.
   - Allow the document to be formatted using existing styles.
   - Don't allow users to change themes or style sets.
3. Close the document, then open it to test your settings.
4. Add comments to the document, specifying what you feel should be added or changed.
5. Save the document in multiple formats.
   - Choose at least one file format that is compatible with other word-processing software.
   - Choose at least one fixed file format.
   - If a format doesn't allow your current security restrictions or other features, discard incompatible content, as necessary.
6. Open each new file you created in Word or its own viewer. Compare its formatting and features with the original.
7. Close all open files.

Alphabetical Index

AutoText..30
Backstage View...122, 131
    Email...131
    Export...122
    Share...122, 131
Blog posts...134, 135
    Creating...135
    Publishing...134
    Registering accounts......................................134
Blogs...135
    Posting to..135
Borders...46
    Page...46
Building blocks..30
    Inserting...30
Captions...95
    Adding..95
Character formatting...63
    Clearing..63
Comments..140, 141, 142
    Adding..141
    Deleting..141
    Displaying..142
    Editing..141
    Inserting..141
Compatibility Mode...135
Cover pages...30
Document properties......................................126
Document restrictions..................146, 147, 149, 150
    Access passwords..147
    Editing...149, 150
    Finalizing documents....................................147
    Formatting..149, 150
Endnote..79, 80
    Change format..80
    Convert to footnote..79
    Modify style...80
    Options...79
Endnotes...79
    Inserting...79
Equations..30
File...130
    Importing..130
    Types...130
File types.......................................122, 124, 128, 135
    Blog posts..135
    PDF..128
    XPS..128
Find..109
    Advanced options..109
    Options...109
Find and Replace..109
Font window...54
Footers..30, 38
    Inserting..30
    Linking..38
Footnote..79, 80
    Change format..80

Convert to endnote..79
Modify style..80
Options...79
Footnotes..79
    Inserting...79
Formatting..54
    Fonts...54
Headers..30, 38
    Inserting...30
    Linking...38
    Linking between sections..............................38
Hyperlinks...101
    Applying..101
    Creating..101
    Options...101
    Types...101
Importing files..130
Keyboard shortcut..58
    Assigning...58
Markup...140, 142
    Comments...140
Master document...115
    Outline view..115
    Outlining tab...115
Metadata..126
Micro formatting toolbar....................................5
Navigation...108, 111, 112
    By object..111
    Document...108
    Document elements......................................112
    Go To...111
    Objects...112
New Style button..60
Nonbreaking space..55
Page backgrounds..........................43, 44, 46, 48
    Borders..46
    Colors...44
    Sections...48
    Watermarks..44
Page colors..44
Page numbers...30
    Inserting...30
Paragraph styles..70
    Defining...70
Paste options..65
Paste Special..66
PDF and XPS documents................................128
Protected View...135
Protection.....................................146, 147, 149, 150
    Editing and formatting restrictions......149, 150
    Finalizing documents....................................147
    Password encryption....................................147
Review pane...142
Saving...128
    Export pane...128
    PDF..128
Saving documents..124
    Export pane...124

Alphabetical Index

Save As 124
Saving files 122
    File types 122
Section breaks 36
    Continuous 36
    Inserting 36
    Odd or even 36
Sections 35, 36, 38, 48
    Changing layout 36
    Headers and footers 38
    Page backgrounds 48
    Setting page numbers 36
Security 135
    Protected View 135
Sending files 131, 133
    Email 131
    Fax 131
    OneDrive 133
    PDF/XPS attachment 131
Shape 8
    Text on a 8
Shape effects 6
Shape fill 6
Shape outline 6
Shape styles 6
Shapes 4, 5, 95
    Adding captions to 95
    Dragging 5
    Insert 4
    Preserving aspect ratio 5
    Resizing 5
Shapes gallery 4
SmartArt 15
    Formatting 15
SmartArt text 15
    Creating sublevels 15
Style Sets 25
    Creating 25
    Saving 25
Styles 57, 58, 60, 63, 72
    Based upon relationship 72
    Creating by example 58

Creating new 63
Defining 60
Heading levels 72
Modifying 63
Types 57
Subdocument 115
    Inserting 115
Subdocuments 116
    Expanding/collapsing 116
    Organizing 116
Table of contents 84, 86, 87, 88
    Automatic 84
    Creating 84
    Customizing 84, 87
    Inserting fields 86
    Manual 84
    Modifying 87
    Options 84
    Planning 86
    Styles 87
    Updating 88
Table of figures 94, 95, 96
    Captions 94, 95
    Inserting 94, 96
Text 8, 110
    Alignment 8
    Direction of 8
    On a shape 8
    Replacing 110
Text box 9
    Inserting onto a shape 9
Text effects 11
Text fill 11
Text outline 11
Themes 22, 23, 24, 25
    Colors 23
    Custom 22
    Elements 22
    Fonts 24
    Managing 25
Watermarks 44
Wildcards 109